ASTON MARTIN V-8

ASTON MARTIN V-8

Michael Bowler

Arco Publishing, Inc.
NEW YORK

Published 1985 by Arco Publishing, Inc.
215 Park Avenue South, New York, NY 10003

Library of Congress Cataloging in Publication Data
Bowler, Michael.
    Aston Martin V-8.

    (High performance series)
    1. Aston Martin automobile. I. Title. II. Series.
TL215.A75B68 1985   629.2'222   84-20411
ISBN 0-668-06428-5

Filmset by Photocomp Limited, Birmingham
Printed and bound in Great Britain
by Biddles of Guildford.

CONTENTS

Pre-War Days 1

Enter David Brown 12

Racing Days 28

Trendsetter GT 50

Racing improves the Breed 69

More Space Less Speed 81

Heart of a V-8 104

Space and Speed 133

New Blood 147

Transfusion 161

Refinement 187

Return to Racing 201

Once more into the breach 223

Author's Preface

Hindsight is a luxury that affords selective coordination of random events. Thus it is with hindsight that I can now link the many associations that have led me towards Aston Martin.

My father, an engineer and amateur Brooklands racer in a 3-litre Bentley, was the post-war competition secretary of the Vintage Sports Car Club so I was able to take a close interest in racing the moment such activities restarted after the war. At that time he was running a 3½-litre Lagonda which was to be replaced by a 2-litre Speed Model Aston. His engineering partner, my godfather Dudley Sidney, ran a DB2. The first motoring journalist I met while seated by the sunny start-line of a VSCC Prescott was S. C. H. Davis, whose initials my older son later shared; at that time I had just saved up to buy the post-war reprint of Sammy's *Racing Motorist*; a Bentley man yes, but also an Aston Martin team member. It was reading and re-reading that book that generated an affinity for Le Mans which I first visited in 1960 when the DBR1s were still running.

As a technical journalist for *Motor* magazine and later as Editor of *Classic Car* magazine, Newport Pagnell was the factory I visited most often. During those seventeen years of motoring journalism I managed to drive just about every model of Aston Martin; those that I hadn't driven before I caught up with when I joined Victor Gauntlett at Pace Petroleum, the month after he had taken over as Joint Chairman of Aston Martin. Although I stayed based at Farnham with Pace I was inevitably involved with Astons in their extramural pursuits, the Pace-linked sponsorships and the Nimrods; by the time I joined Astons full-time in October 1983 I already knew many of the people involved and was well versed in the spirit that has kept the old firm afloat despite so many adversities. Neither my father nor godfather are now around to see the outcome of any thoughts they might subconsciously have implanted, but I am grateful to them and to Victor for steering me towards the home of the best of British cars.

I actually undertook to write this book before leaving Pace Petroleum but the pressure of life at Newport Pagnell has slowed progress somewhat. Once there I have had the good fortune to have access to many of the original reports of work undertaken at the factory (and Feltham before it) from 1960 to the present day; I am grateful to those who compiled those reports, but almost more so to those who have preserved so many of them.

Foreword

by Victor Gauntlett

Executive Chairman Aston Martin Lagonda Limited

Reading Michael Bowler's book one cannot fail to be aware of the depth of history that lies behind our current product range. It is the history of a company that has produced thoroughbred after thoroughbred, proven on the track as well as on the road.

The challenge of continuing such a great tradition would test the very fibre of any company, let alone one that has had to deal with so many crises during its seventy year history.

It is a tribute to many that Aston Martin has met that challenge and supported in the fullest sense the cause of the thoroughbred in motoring. Among the men who helped create this beautiful car Lionel Martin was responsible for its conception and Bert Bertelli, the Sutherlands, David Brown, Peter Sprague and Alan Curtis were responsible for its production during their stewardship of the company.

The challenge becomes more demanding as the years go by, particularly the financial implications of a new model and for this reason Aston Martin and its many supporters should be much encouraged by the involvement of my fellow shareholders, the Livanos family, who are providing a degree of support that has just not been available before, but which is vital to fuel what will be an exciting future.

It can be no surprise that I take a great deal of pleasure and pride in being at the helm of this very special company, but I am conscious of the enormous responsibility of helping to guide it into the 1990's with a product range that the likes of Harold Beach, Tadek Marek, John Wyer, Frank Feeley and Williams Towns and their teams would have approved.

I regard the current range of Aston Martin as true lineal descendants of the cars of W. O. Bentley, not just through Bentley's involvement in Lagondas both before and after the war, but because of their essential character: Bentley and Aston Martin Lagonda set out to build Kings of the Road in their day. We will seek nothing less for the future of our marque.

Inevitably I have read most of the books that have so far been written about Aston Martin but I must make particular reference to those that covered the post-war scene in such detail. Foremost among these is John Wyer whose books, *Racing with the David Brown Aston Martins* (published by Transport Bookman) and *The Certain Sound* (published by Automobile Year), give so much background to the bald facts of racing results and factory production. I count myself fortunate to have known John Wyer since his Gulf GT40 days and am proud to follow, albeit very remotely, in the nearest available path to his footsteps.

Dudley Gershon's book, *Aston Martin 1963-72* (published by Oxford Illustrated Press), gave me continuity from the Wyer period and the inside story behind factory decisions of the time. For the background to Touring Superleggera I must acknowledge the book of that name by Anderloni and Anselmi (published by Autocritica).

While Aston Martin enjoys a great reputation, the company is very fortunate in having had such a stalwart Owners Club to keep the flag flying throughout all the ups and downs, and to foster the enthusiasm of the various shareholders. The AMOC has had the continuity since 1935 to maintain almost factory records and the club's annual register is a mine of information on facts and figures. Likewise the club's publication *Aston Martin Quarterly*, edited so interestingly for many years by Brian Joscelyne, is full of pertinent interviews and stories from Aston's many past characters. I feel it is appropriate that this book should be published in the AMOC's Golden Jubilee year.

I must close the acknowledgements by thanking many of my present colleagues who have allowed themselves to be distracted from the serious business of modern car production to answer my random questions on past events; it is a measure of the company's spirit that there are still so many people around who can recall working for 'DB'.

It was a great pleasure for me recently to take part in the same convoy as Sir David Brown as we drove from Aston dealer Chapman-Spooner to the centre of Birmingham; I was in a DB4GT while Sir David was in the passenger's seat of a DBR1, the first time, since he drove the winning car from Le Mans to La Chartre, that he had sat in one. Thank you then to all Aston Martin enthusiasts throughout the world who have supported the factory through thick and thin; I hope this book gives you a little more insight into some of the history behind your enthusiasm.

Michael Bowler, Heronsgate, Herts. October 1984.

Chapter One

Pre-War Days

In the beginning was Aston Clinton with Lionel Martin and Robert Bamford. On May 9th, 1914 Lionel Martin won, on handicap, a timed ½-mile hill-climb which took place on the gentle slopes of the Chiltern Hills in Buckinghamshire. The car he used was a Singer modified for performance by Lionel Martin and his partner Robert Bamford in the company they had set up the year before as Bamford and Martin.

On October 19th, 1914 *Light Car and Cyclecar* said that it was an open secret that Mr. Martin was designing his own car which would be called an Aston Martin; one of their staff men rode in the prototype, an Isotta Fraschini chassis powered by a Coventry Simplex 4-cylinder of 1388cc.

Double-barrelled names had become established as highly marketable with such as Rolls-Royce, Hispano-Suiza, Delaunay-Belleville, Alfa-Romeo, Lorraine-Dietrich, Sheffield-Simplex aiming at the top of the tree. Mr. Martin's new car could so easily have been called a Martin Bamford or a Bamford Clinton, but they chose wisely and well – Aston Martin it was to be.

However, the Great War (1914-18) put a stop to further work and it was not until 1920 that the second car was built, still with a side-valve engine now increased to 1486cc, the better to compete and prove the marque in voiturette racing. Bamford resigned that year, his place as director taken by Mrs. Martin in their new premises in West Kensington.

The desire to prove their cars in racing was pre-eminent in the minds of the Martins, but a production rate of a car a month for four years was not producing the wherewithal to take to the tracks. But during that time Aston Martin went to Le Mans for the first time, albeit for the Coupé des Voiturettes where Bugattiste B. S. Marshall finished sixth in

1

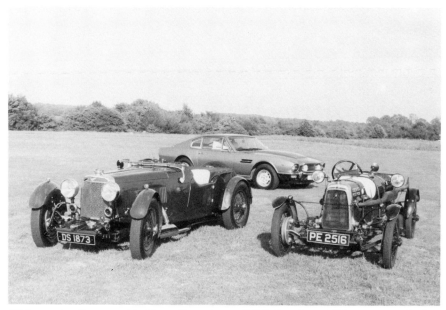

Wide ranging line-up with Green Pea – the ex-1922 Strasbourg GP car renamed when its side valve engine was fitted in 1923 – alongside a 1933 Le Mans 2/4 seater with the 1978 AMV-8 demonstrator behind.

a side-valve Aston. That same year, 1921, saw four Astons run in the inaugural JCC 200-mile race where Marshall's side-valve car beat Count Zborowski in another Aston, now powered by a 16-valve four-cylinder designed by Robb – ninth and tenth were the best they managed though.

The Count had acquired a financial interest in Aston Martin and obviously saw it as a means of continuing racing; not happy with the performance of the Robb 16-valve engine, Zborowski sent Clive Gallop to acquire a revised head from a former Peugeot designer; two cars thus powered impressed, but failed to finish at the 1922 Strasbourg GP. George Eyston managed to finish fourth the following year but that was the best that the 16-valve units ever mustered in International competition; the side-valves continued to show greater reliability.

By the time of Count Zborowski's death in a Mercedes at the 1924 Italian Grand Prix, the Hon. John Benson had also become involved in keeping Aston Martin afloat. Only 50 Astons had been produced prior to the company's first Motor Show attendance in October 1925, but whatever promise of sales there may have been, the company was declared insolvent a month later. John Benson was now in charge of the remains at a time when William Renwick and Augustus Bertelli were forming a partnership to produce engines for the motor industry, and possibly complete cars as well. Bertelli had come from Enfield Alldays and it was into one of their cars that Bertelli's new overhead camshaft 1½-litre four was inserted.

Bertelli had met Martin through racing and obviously decided that it was simpler to step into Aston Martin than continue with his own company. Renwick and Bertelli moved from their Birmingham premises down to Feltham, forming Aston Martin Motors in October 1925, with Benson joining them there.

A year later, by which time Bertelli's brother Enrico had also moved to Feltham, the first of the new line was launched. This continued the basic theme of producing 1½-litre two-to-four seater open bodies for the fairly wealthy enthusiast. £465 was the price of the chassis which could be delivered in 8ft 6in and 9ft 6in wheelbase forms, the latter very long for a car of this size, but it was chosen to get four people seated

The ex-Zborowski 1922 Strasbourg GP car with its 16-valve engine seen here at a 1951 AMOC meeting flanked by a pair of Le Mans 2/4 seaters.

3

between the wheels and keep the roof height of the saloon as low as possible.

Once again competition thoughts loomed, and, in 1928, two cars were sent to the Le Mans 24-hour race – LM1 and LM2. Lightened and with the longevity of their overhead camshaft engines improved by dry sump lubrication – to keep oil temperatures down – the cars didn't finish, but Bertelli, driving with record breaker George Eyston, was seventh when they stopped after 350 miles. However, the experience

Bert Bertelli seen many years after he held the Aston Martin reins from 1926-35.

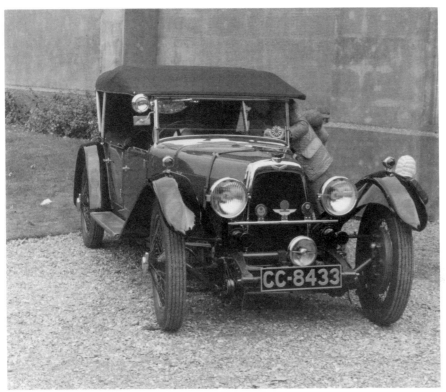

The 14th of Bertelli's production cars was this 4-seater Tourer of 1928.

gained was put to good use as the dry sump version of the International was announced the same year.

But 1929 was to be the start of the world depression and the next two years saw many companies in trouble. In fact, Aston Martin more or less weathered the worst of the storm, but even 130 cars sold between 1928 and 1931 was not enough when they were so expensive to manufacture with arguably needless production of items which could more effectively be bought from outside. Both Benson and Renwick had earlier left the two Bertellis but, despite further injection from both southern Aston distributor L. Prideaux Brune and, surprisingly, Frazer Nash manufacturers AFN, the company was once again put on the market at the end of 1931.

The new owner was to be Sir Arthur Sutherland, a baronet, with 'Bert' Bertelli remaining a director, along with Sir Arthur's son Gordon, who was to run the company although still only in his twenties.

5

Gleaming engine of a 1½-litre Mk. II distinguished by the thermostatically controlled radiator shutters. Engine is single overhead camshaft with dry sump lubrication, the oil tank being between the dumb-irons.

Le Mans 1934 with LM11/12/14 carrying numbers 21/2/3; LM10 is number 20 competing in its third Le Mans to finish tenth. LM7 (No. 24) was also on its third event and finished fifteenth.

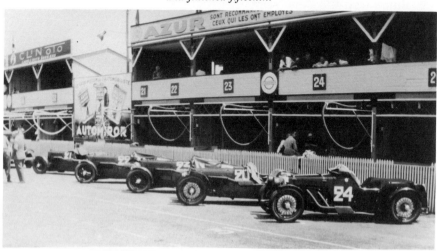

For 1933 the cars were using Laycock gearboxes directly attached to the engine and ENV spiral bevel rear axles, rather than their own remote gearboxes and worm drive axles. Prices came down, the four-door saloon on the 10ft wheelbase dropping from £745 to £595 and the Le Mans 2/4 seater from £650 to £595; Frazer Nash was selling its two-seater TT Replica at £445 with a proprietary Meadows engine and its unique transmission.

The brochure defined 'Our Objects'.

In continuing the production of these cars, our object is to keep available to the public at least one car which has not been affected by the general cuts in prices and workmanship which have taken place in recent years. We believe that there are still discriminating motorists in existence who can appreciate the finer points in the handling of a motor car. For these we have marketed our Le Mans model, and are confident that they will find in it a unique vehicle which will handle better and give them more confidence than any other in existence.

Classic Ulster lines with the painted grille and the tail fared to cover a horizontal spare wheel; this is the last of the production Ulsters.

Saloon elegance on a long wheelbase Mk. II chassis; lack of rear wheel intrusion allows a proper four-seater under a low roof-line.

In conclusion, may we add that we honestly believe that our car is unrivalled in its class and it is our aim to try and offer to all Aston Martin owners not only an unrivalled car, but also service and personal attention in keeping with it. With this end in view we run a specialised Service Department and do our utmost to add this very desirable attribute to an already noteworthy car.' With only minor adjustments to language the same is as true today as it was fifty years ago.

Despite those eulogies afforded the 1933 cars, the following year saw the Mk. II introduced with a stronger chassis of varying depth, and the distinguishing feature of thermostatically controlled shutters in front of the radiator. In its most sporting form, the engine, with twin SU carburettors, produced 70bhp at 4750rpm; the brochure highlights the fact that the dry sump system circulates two gallons of oil a minute at 3000rpm and even in racing conditions *'it is impossible to raise the oil temperature above 75°C.'* Further, *'the Aston Martin engine can be driven indefinitely at 4000rpm . . . . actually the engine will run up to over 5000rpm . . . .'*

In a 19cwt car this gave pretty good performance for its day with a maximum around 85mph. The chassis was priced at £535 with its elegant 2/4 seater version on the 8ft 7in chassis totalling £610. Given a 10ft wheelbase, the 4-seater open car was £640 and the 2-door sports saloon with sliding sun-roof came to £700. By contrast the Lagonda 2-litre saloon was £695, a Riley 12/6 saloon £350, a Riley MPH £550, while the MG Magnette Airline coupé was £385.

The recipe was obviously nearly right as there were 166 Mk. IIs produced between 1934 and 1936. By then Gordon Sutherland wanted to soften the cars still further. Before he left the company Bertelli had, however, produced his masterpiece, the Ulster.

This 15/98 2-litre with its wet sump engine was the subject of the August 1938 Motor *Road test. It is seen here undergoing testing at Brooklands; the body was by Abbey Coachworks.*

Claude Hill (right) visiting the factory at an AMOC open day Newport Pagnell in 1977; after he left Aston Martin he went to work for Harry Ferguson until 1971. Here he is talking to Inman Hunter, historian and author on early Astons, who joined Aston Martin as an apprentice in 1931.

A classic case of what looks right is right, the Ulster was ultra low, its heavily louvred bonnet stretching back from a painted radiator shell, horizontal exhaust system with a Brooklands can silencer running back into a fish tail which gave the now 80bhp engine a characteristic crackle, a shapely pointed tail fared out at the bottom to engulf a horizontal spare wheel; with slim cycle wings, quick-action petrol filler caps, a battery of aircraft switches and a couple of aero screens, it looked the part. For £750 you had a guaranteed 100mph car too. The 17 production cars were replicas of the four team cars of 1934; while these had failed to finish at Le Mans when painted green, three in Bertelli's Italian red took third, sixth and seventh in the same year's Tourist Trophy in Ulster, winning the team prize and justification for a new model name.

Sutherland's new cars came under the design influence of Claude Hill, Bertelli's assistant. The engine was considerably revised with larger bore and stroke to give 2-litres; intake and exhaust were switched and the standard 16/98 no longer had dry sump lubrication. However, the Speed Model retained its dry sump and, as shades of things to come perhaps, the brochure merely said *'well over 100bhp is available and the engine is safe to 5500rpm'*. As before a full range of bodywork was offered with prices ranging from £575 for the open cars to £775 for the Speed Model, whether with attractive two-plus-two open bodywork, or the controversial C-type which suffered from an over-bulbous front end. Certainly the 16/98s were comfortable to drive, more so than the earlier cars, but they retained more of the Aston character than Bertelli's sudden departure would have implied.

Although the new cars were selling quite well, Sutherland and Hill started work on an all-new car using virtually a space frame for its four-door streamlined saloon bodywork; front suspension followed the Porsche designed Auto-Union trailing arms while the rear used a live axle on leaf springs. Its engine had to catch up later as the company became an engineering sub-contractor to the war-effort; this all-new Claude Hill design, a four cylinder 2-litre of shorter stroke but with push-rod overhead valves, was to be the basis of post-war production.

Chapter Two

Enter David Brown

Post-war, as time and thought again returned to motor cars, Sutherland and Hill were not ready to launch straight into the market with the new car; it needed considerable money. Accordingly, the company was put up for sale.

One who acted when he saw the advertisement was David Brown, industrialist. His grandfather had started a pattern-making business in 1860; David Brown's father succeeded him and brought the gear production side of the business in from Germany. David Brown joined his father and, when barely thirty, expanded the company into production of the Harry Ferguson tractors. The company had motoring connections through the provision of superchargers for Amherst Villiers, both for Raymond Mays' Vauxhall-Villiers and the blower Bentleys, and David Brown had a strong personal interest.

Brown visited the Feltham factory, drove the streamlined Atom saloon and bought the company, Gordon Sutherland and Claude Hill remaining with it. Following the chairman's edict, an open version of the Atom was created complete with Hill's 2-litre push-rod engine; however, the rear suspension was changed for more positive location with trailing arms and a Panhard rod with coil springs. Some 15 of these were to be produced by the end of 1950, but it was the prototype that captured the imagination. With a special lightweight body, the car was driven to victory in the 1948 Spa 24-hour race at 72.1mph in the hands of St. John Horsfall and Leslie Johnson. The Brown philosophy, as with Martin, Bertelli and to a lesser extent Sutherland, was to prove such cars as Astons in racing, especially long distance road racing, where reliability rather than sheer speed was paramount. However, David Brown was not one to be happy with perpetual class wins and sought

Leslie Johnson co-driving with Jock St. John Horsfall won the 1948 Spa 24-hours using Claude Hill's 2-litre engine in the DB1 chassis. Racing proved the breed.

outright victory. Accordingly, Claude Hill started to design a 6-cylinder version of his pushrod 2-litre. Fate, however, had other ideas.

Lagonda had a longer heritage than did Aston Martin. American, Wilbur Gunn, from Lagonda, Ohio, emigrated to England before the turn of the century, setting up in Staines, Middlesex to build motorcycles. Tricars followed in 1904. Then came the 20hp Torpedo in 1906, next a 4-cylinder which took Gunn and Bert Hammond to victory in the 1910 Moscow-St Petersburg Reliability Trial, forming a Russian export market in the process, which lasted until the outbreak of war.

Meanwhile, Gunn had some financial problem, but remained at the helm. A new 11.1hp light car came in 1913 with a rivetted monocoque chassis; post-war it became the 11.9, then 12/24. Lagonda moved into the sports-car market with the 14/60 using a 2-litre four-cylinder with hemispherical combustion chamber and twin high camshafts; 2½ and 3-litre pushrod engines followed to power these full four-seater fast tourers. Gunn died at the end of the First War, but the company carried on with the existing directors.

An 1100cc dohc Rapier appeared in 1933 together with the 4½-litre

13

Despite the 1948 success no-one wanted to buy Spa replicas; here the Spa car has been rebuilt for the 1948 Motor Show.

Meadows-engined M45. However, financial problems were again looming but Alan Good arrived to save the company from being taken over by Rolls-Royce; he promptly appointed W. O. Bentley, whose company was absorbed by Rolls in 1931, as chief designer. While this was happening Lagonda managed to win the 1935 Le Mans with a Rapide version of the M45.

Good and Bentley proceeded to improve the existing cars, introducing the LG45 with greater comfort and more apparent luxury with Bentley's improved version of the Meadows 4½ coming in 1936. A year later came the 4½-litre V-12 drawn up by Stuart Tresilian under Bentley's direction; it was a magnificent unit, very flexible and utterly suited to the luxury market for which Lagondas were now produced. Frank Feeley had been with Lagonda for some ten years and was responsible for the rounded elegance of their coachwork. Rapide versions were third and fourth at Le Mans in the final event of the pre-war era.

During the war Lagonda was engaged in munitions, but was ready with a new car in 1945. With input from W. O. Bentley, William Watson and Donald Bastow it was a superb conception, a luxury four/ five seater with a 2½-litre twin overhead camshaft six-cylinder unit, the LB6. The cruciform chassis was suspended on wishbones at the front and a swing axle at the rear, with coil springs at the front and long torsion bars at the rear. A separate steel monocoque was laid on top of the chassis to take the home-grown bodywork still under the eye of Frank Feeley. The new car was launched in the press in September 1945 with production expected to start the following year. In calling the car a Lagonda-Bentley, Good incurred the wrath of Rolls, then as now very protective of their trade name rights: a lost lawsuit and cars still not in production led Good to put Lagonda up for sale.

It was an approach by one of Lagonda's northern distributors that set David Brown on the Lagonda trail to find that Rootes and Jaguar were also interested, with offers up to £250,000. However, the poor

Only 15 DB1 chassis were built; this is the first one with the production bodywork, a lot for a 2-litre to pull around.

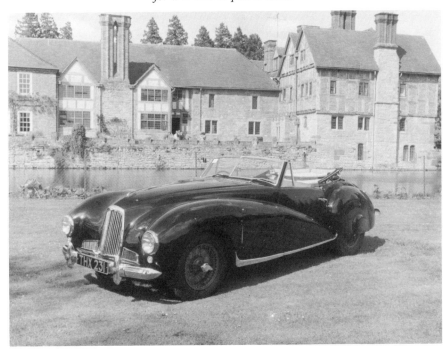

Much of Aston Martin work was carried out at David Brown's other factories; here DB2
engines are assembled at Farsley, Yorks.

economic outlook deterred them and Brown finally bought the
company, but not its premises, for £52,500. Brown had already decided
that Aston Martin couldn't afford to put Hill's new 6-cylinder engine
into production from scratch, and realised, after trying the Lagonda
prototype, that it already possessed the power unit for which he was
looking.

In fact the Lagonda was not to go into production until 1949, and in
improved form would continue alongside the Astons to 1957, in 3-litre
form for the last four years.

So what was special about the engine that David Brown had bought?
Put simply, it was a cast-iron six-cylinder of 2580cc with twin chain-
driven overhead camshafts producing over 100bhp. From his previous
experience W. O. determined to provide crankcase rigidity and good
water circulation around bores and valve areas. This was achieved with
a deep well-ribbed block/crankcase for which the crankshaft was fed

The fourth DB2 was built in 1949 and used as a works development car; Lance Macklin took 2nd place in the 1950 Inter Europa Cup at Monza. Outlet grille behind front wheelarch uses simple louvres at this stage.

through a hole in the back, leaving the bottom face completely flat for better sump sealing; cast iron wet liners ensured good water circulation. The crankshaft used four main bearings; at the front a steel-backed shell was inserted in the crankcase; the other three used a system of 'cheeses' – half a circular aluminium casting mated to its opposite half while the crank was being fed through; once in they were located by hollow dowels through which the oil passed. Being of aluminium the cheeses were easily assembled into a cold cast-iron unit, but would expand to a tight fit with the engine warm.

The stroke of 90mm was chosen as slightly longer than that for the V-12 and to give overlap of big end and main bearing pins for rigidity, given 2-inch pin diameters. Forged connecting rods included buttress webs from H-section to little and big end and a webbed bearing cap, again for the sake of rigidity. The hemispherical valve layout was chosen to ensure water circulation around the exhaust valve, and the valve guides were also wet to help this; the good breathing of such a layout also ensured flexibility with over 100psi bmep available from 500 to 5000rpm.

Camshafts were chain driven via a jack-shaft which drove the water pump with a separate, and thus shorter than usual, chain running to the camshafts. Valves were directly operated via bucket tappets. Eschewing the usual pedestal bearings for camshafts, W. O.s ran in semi-circular cups in the top head face with aluminium bearing caps on top; each cam was supported by a bearing on each side.

It was a sophisticated and well thought-out unit with plenty of potential, ideal for what David Brown had in mind for Aston Martin – to make the world's best sporting Grand Tourer. Perhaps sadly, Claude Hill left shortly afterwards. However, Hill's legacy was the chassis which was a further development of the Atom with the rear axle now controlled laterally by a Watt linkage. With the LB6 engine mated to a David Brown gearbox, the car was then aluminium clad by another Frank Feeley masterpiece. The DB2 was born as a striking two-seater with luggage platform behind and the spare wheel fed through a slot in the tail.

This fifth DB2 was finished in 1950 and was originally fitted with the 2-litre engine but became the 2.6-litre development vehicle.

Three of these cars made a racing debut at Le Mans in 1949, one with the LB6 and two with Hill's 2-litre. Unfortunately, the 'six' retired earlier with a water pump defect, and one of the 'fours' crashed, but the other finished seventh. Two weeks later the 'six' finished third in the Spa 24 hours.

Thus the DB2 was launched in the spring of 1950 with 105bhp; the 125bhp Vantage version followed at the end of the year, by which time there was also a drophead DB2. 1950 also saw the arrival of three significant people at Feltham, two of them already known figures. John Wyer joined in March with a racing background, most recently with Monaco Motors, Watford, who were specialists at preparing racing machinery, including a rival Aston at the 1948 Spa 24 hours. He took on the post of Team Manager for the racing and Development Engineer. Le Mans 1950 saw two cars finish in fifth and sixth places overall, in the hands of Lance Macklin and George Abecassis who also won the 3-litre class and the Index of Performance.

Hand assembly methods applied to one of the early DB2 development cars.

19

Late in 1950 David Brown brought in the Austrian engineer, Eberan von Eberhorst who had made a name with Auto-Union pre-war with Dr. Porsche, stayed with them post-war for the ill-fated Cisitalia Grand Prix car and then come to England to work with ERA. It was through the latter that he met David Brown, who brought him to Feltham as Chief Designer.

The third significant figure to join in 1950 was Harold Beach as a Design Draughtsman; he had been through Barkers the coach-builders before the war, followed by Beardmore, then an engineering sub-contract firm for Rolls-Royce numbering among its achievements the body design for Eddie Hall's 3½-litre Bentley. After a wartime spell on airfield test equipment, he saw an advertisement in 1950 for design draughtsman for David Brown Tractors (Engineering) Automobile Division at Feltham. All the drawings of that period were on David Brown Tractors' paper. Harold Beach started work on designing the

Le Mans 1950 and three cars were entered. This car driven by Brackenbury/Parnell finished sixth, Macklin/Abecassis were fifth and Thompson/Gordon broke a crankshaft after 8 laps.

Early customer in 1951 was Lord Brabazon of Tara seen here with David Brown alongside chassis 88. The production cars lost the louvred outlets of the development vehicles and established the definitive Feeley DB2 shape.

The spare wheel was installed horizontally through the rear trap door while luggage was loaded through the side door. Here George Abecassis plays a rather self-conscious male model with Angela Brown, the boss's daughter whom he married.

Using a rather special DB2 Lindon Sims and Tony Ambrose won the 1956 RAC Rally.

In a sole works foray into the Monte Carlo rally, Astons entered three DB2/4s. Gatsonides/Becquart would have won but for a missed secret check, but Parnell/ Klementaski (here) and Collins/G. Whitehead found the road sections too boring and lost many marks, Collins redeeming the situation by winning the round-the-houses race.

The DB2/4 was introduced in October 1953 with chassis changes to allow two occasional rear seats with luggage access through the first proper hatchback. Slight hunchback did not detract from the DB2's lines. The Mk. II followed in October 1955.

Functionally informative, the DB2/4 facia was readily adaptable to left hand drive form.

The DB2/4 Mk. II came in this fixed head coupé form as well as continuing the DB2 theme; bonnet break was now above the chrome side strip rather than lifting the whole front end.

Mk. II bodywork was made at Tickford's Newport Pagnell factory now owned by David Brown.

Marek redesigned the 3-litre VB6 engine under DP164, with stiffer crankcase, new crankshaft and manifolds, to give 162bhp at 5500rpm in this twin SU form, as the DBA.

DB2's successor, which was to be the DB3. Two years later his work was all undone by von Eberhorst who had his own fixed ideas and the DB3 was to become purely a racing machine.

The DB2 was to last until 1953, by which time its successor had become the DB2/4, stretched slightly and with the rear cross-member altered to allow two small seats while the luggage platform access was through a top-hinged rear door, the true forerunner of the hatchback. Additional rear headroom meant sacrificing some of the original looks but it was a good and successful compromise; the 2.6-litre engines were now producing 125bhp for all models before a bore increase gave 2.9-litre in 1954 for 140bhp at 5000rpm, enough for a maximum speed of just under 120mph.

Initially the DB2/4 bodies were built by Mulliners while the Lagondas went to Tickford, Newport Pagnell. Tickford was then added to the David Brown empire in 1955 and the DB2/4 bodies went there; meanwhile, with production at five or so cars a week, Feltham had been

Mk. III adopted an intake shape similar to that of the DB3S. This car finished first in class in the 1959 Monte Carlo Rally with Count de Salis/Bridgeman.

Rear seats were still pretty nominal but a raised roof line gave a little more headroom on the Mk. III.

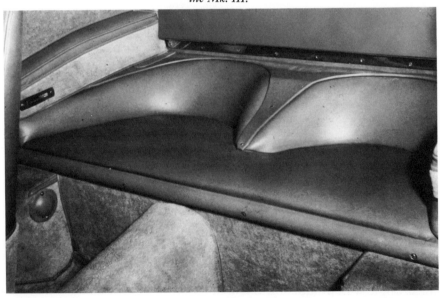

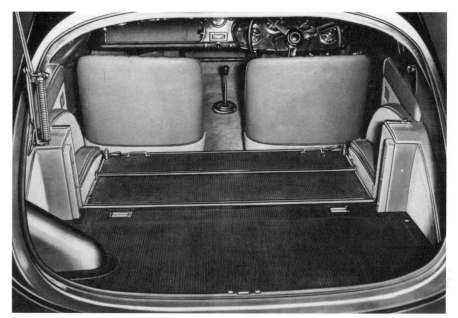

The DB2/4 Mk. III or just DB Mk. III had the new one-piece facia grouped around the steering wheel which was to continue as an Aston hallmark. Seats down shows remarkable luggage space.

outgrown, and much of the engineering production was carried out at Farsley in Yorkshire. This was moved to Newport Pagnell in 1956. By this time von Eberhorst had gone and John Wyer had been Technical Director for two years; passing the daily involvement of the racing management to Reg Parnell, Wyer now became General Manager at a time when the DB2/4 was beginning to lose its sales appeal; 411 of the first DB2 had been built, followed by 565 DB2/4s in two years; then came the Mk. II with minor revisions with a Vantage version now giving 165bhp; but only 199 were built in the 1½ years up to Spring 1957.

Profiting from race exprience the engine had been considerably developed and redesignated DBA with new block/crankshaft and camshafts to produce 162bhp in twin SU form. This was inserted into the DB2/4 Mk. III and DB Mk. III, which had an intake grille resembling that of the DB3S. It was this model that Wyer was able to sell on his world-wide sales tour in 1957 as a means of bridging the financial gap until the arrival of the DB4. The strategy worked, just, and the Mk. III in its saloon, coupé and open forms continued in production alongside the first year of DB4s.

Chapter Three

Racing Days

For David Brown the best way of promoting high performance road cars, and proving their components first, was to go racing; this philosophy dictated much of his thinking and the people he employed.

The DB2s were already there when John Wyer joined and his first success at Le Mans had already been recorded. During the rest of that year DB2s came 2, 3, 4 in the 3-litre class of the production Car Race at Silverstone, being beaten on a damp track by Duncan Hamilton in a Silverstone Healey, and 1, 2, 3 in the 3-litre class at the Tourist Trophy at Dundrod. However, von Eberhorst was hard at work designing the DB3 to be the mainstay of 1951 competition. The basic brief was to build a completely new car around the LB6 2.6-litre engine. While the use of a cast-iron engine in a racing car set its own handicap, it was essential from the production proving viewpoint. Von Eberhorst was more theoretician than pragmatist and determined to develop his designs on the drawing board rather than on the track, with the result that the DB3 wasn't ready to run until the end of the 1951 season. Fortunately, Wyer had assessed the situation correctly and built a pair of lightweight DB2s using thinner gauge bodywork and drilled chassis; shorn of all unnecessary weight they scaled some 4cwt less than the 1950 Le Mans cars. After a trial run at Silverstone, where Parnell won the 3-litre class, with aluminium cylinder heads, the team set off for Le Mans with the two lightweight cars and the 1950 fifth place car lightened, using cast iron heads again but with Weber carburetters and 138bhp. It was a great success and they finished third, fifth and seventh with privateers tenth and thirteenth to record a 100 per cent finish. The cars also recorded 1, 2, 3 in the 3-litre class with the highest finisher being the lightened 1950 car.

Meanwhile, work continued on the DB3. Eberhorst had followed his Auto-Union practice to a large extent with a twin-tube ladder frame chassis, trailing arm front suspension and de Dion rear located by radius arms and a Panhard rod, with transverse torsion bars and inboard rear brake drums. Just a single car was ready for the TT, its unpainted slab-sided Feeley bodywork characterised by that portcullis grille; in the event it lost its oil through the last minute adoption of a magnesium sump, instead of steel, which allowed the clamping screws to loosen through differential expansion. One of the lightweight DB2s salvaged a seventh place.

The DB3 had shown that it could work but its handling needed sorting out. This was achieved over the winter with a trip to Montlhery which revealed a fundamental geometric weakness in the rear suspension. Using non parallel trailing arms presents no problems in purely vertical deflection but, when the car rolls, the arms try to twist the de Dion tube which thus acts as a very stiff torsion bar leading to

As the new competition DB3 was not going to be ready for the 1951 season, John Wyer had a team of two lightweight DB2s built with drilled chassis, plexiglass windows and minimal trim to save 450lb. Reg Parnell poses by the cars XMC 76 and XMC 77.

instant oversteer. While this can be used deliberately in conjunction with appropriately chosen mounting rubbers to allow soft springing for a comfortable ride without generating excessive roll, it was simply a mistake in the DB3 which was cured by making the arms parallel. Aston Martin was of course chasing Jaguar at this time, but 2.6-litre versus 3.4-litres was not a particularly fair contest. Endeavouring to increase the LB6 to 3-litres by overboring was not as simple as it sounds, as each pair of cylinders was bunched into a siamese by the main bearings and there wasn't enough meat in the liners to find the necessary 5mm bore increase. The bores had to be offset which was overcome by offsetting the little end; that this exerted bending loads on the gudgeon pin was amply shown at the 1952 Monaco sports car race when all three DB3s retired with failed rods, although one just crossed the line at the right moment to qualify seventh.

Le Mans that year saw three DB3s back with 2.6 litre engines and all three were out very early on, two with a final drive failure – an isolated problem with the special high ratio – and one with gearbox failure in the special 5-speed gearbox. A disastrous outing. For the final major race of the year, the Goodwood 9-hour, the Parnell/Thompson car had a new 3-litre unit. Unfortunately, that car suffered a final drive oil leak which,

The DB3 chassis followed von Eberhorst's Auto-Union theme of a substantial twin-tube chassis with torsion bar suspension.

This DB3 engine with triple 36DCF Webers was used for most of the 1952 season but was less powerful than with the 35DCO.

when compounded with hot inboard brakes and a dollop of petrol during a pit-stop, promptly caught fire. Three people were burned, two of whom, including John Wyer, were put in hospital for three weeks. Despite that, the Griffiths/Collins DB3 went on to win, salvaging something from an otherwise inglorious season.

Meanwhile, David Brown still wanted an out and out winner of major sports car races, something like a big V-12 to tackle the Ferraris. Accordingly, Willie Watson, who had come from Bentley to be a senior design engineer in 1952, was put onto the design of a 4.5-litre V-12, a totally separate exercise from the previous Lagonda. While W. O. Bentley had learnt from his V-12 in designing the LB6, Watson learnt from the LB6 in creating the next V-12, retaining the threaded crankshaft and main bearing cheese system but with an aluminium block. Lubrication was by dry sump and the double overhead camshaft heads used twin plugs per cylinder. It was an ambitious project which was to take considerable research time at a point when the engineering team was trying hard to develop the DB3 and update the DB2/4.

31

While 1952 was meant to be the year of the DB3 none finished at Le Mans and it was left to this privateer DB2 of Peter Clark/Mike Keen to take seventh place and third in class behind the winning Mercedes 300SLs.

Start of Le Mans 1952 and the Collins/Macklin DB3 leads the Mann/Goodall DB2 with Stoop's Frazer Nash behind. The DB3 went out in the nineteenth hour when third with a failed final drive.

It was to be another 1½-years before the car would take to the track and Watson kept in touch with what was happening around the rest of the 50-strong engineering department. With Jaguar still half a litre ahead, the DB3 needed lightening; Watson approached Wyer with his ideas which were simply to reduce the gauges of the main chassis tubes and cant them downwards to give a lower seating position; Feeley came up with another body-style reverting to a style more curvaceous than that used for the DB3, whose slab sides were reminiscent of Touring bodywork of the late 'thirties, but which probably arose from a decapitated DB2.

Once von Eberhorst had given his approval, which meant accepting that he had over-engineered his own design, work went ahead remarkably quickly, endorsed by David Brown. Most of the rest of the car was carried over from the DB3, of which only 10 were built overall; one alteration though was to change the iron-cased Salisbury hypoid bevel final drive for a David Brown built ali-cased spiral bevel unit which

Boreham in August 1952, where Parnell was third and won the 3-litre class. Here Parnell talks to von Eberhorst.

Pitstop for the Parnell/Thompson DB3S which won the 1953 Goodwood nine hours with Collins/Griffith second. John Wyer has his megaphone poised.

carried central slide location for the de Dion tube.

Progress on the DB3S was not so fast that the team didn't have to start the 1953 season with the DB3. The Sebring 12-hours saw one of the two cars finish second to a Cunningham, the Mille Miglia saw a fifth for Parnell, and Silverstone third and fourth in the Production Sports Race, 3-litre class winners again. By now the 3-litre engine was producing 160bhp on triple 34 DCO Webers.

The DB3S was ready for Le Mans with three new cars: DB3S/2, /3, and /4 for Parnell/Collins, Abecassis/Salvadori and Poore/Thompson. It wasn't an auspicious start for the 3S; new cams and bigger valves improved the output to 182bhp but the cams were machined from steel billets due to lack of time and an associated tappet failure eliminated one car, while Parnell crashed one early on and another had clutch failure from a leaking gearbox seal. However, the new cars were ½-minute faster than the 2.6-litre DB3, which was validated when Astons beat Jaguar in each of the remaining outings, Parnell's solo victory at the Isle of Man Empire Trophy Race, a 1, 2, 3 in the Production race at

Silverstone, a 1, 2 in the Goodwood 9-hours (Parnell the victor in each), finishing with a victory for Collins/Griffiths and second at the TT.

For 1954 work was continuing on the Lagonda which was to prove a dead end; planned for 350bhp, the most it ever achieved was 312bhp because it just couldn't reach the desired 7500rpm; since in almost every respect it followed LB6 design, including the twin plug heads that were to feature in the 1954 DB3S, it seemed to have theory behind it. In practice, the choice of an aluminium block was its undoing; in the LB6 the cheese or diaphragm main bearing housing in aluminium expanded into the cast-iron block to make a firm fit; with the V-12, there was no such differential expansion and the bearings couldn't take the strain.

The engine was, however, inserted into a stretched, and later stengthened version of the DB3S chassis and clad in another attractively curvaceous shape. A fifth and a fourth at Silverstone in 1954

Lagonda V-12 engine in the chassis DP115. The dry sump 4½-litre four-cam unit only achieved 312bhp at 6000rpm; higher revs destroyed the bearings.

Silverstone testing for the Lagonda, looking very Aston from this view. John Wyer emerges.

At the 1955 TT there was no hope of beating the 300SLR Mercedes but Walker/Poore achieved fourth and Parnell/Salvadori (here) seventh, in DB3S/7.

and 1955, a crash at Le Mans in 1954 and an engine failure in 1955, by which time it had a new Watson designed space-frame chassis, were the results of its only races. Their greatest claim to fame was featuring in a Mille-Miglia type film starring James Robertson Justice. At the end of the 1955 season, the Lagonda V-12 was declared dead, and any thoughts of its eventual production use likewise were abandoned.

Von Eberhorst had left the team at the end of 1953 and Wyer was Technical Director. David Brown wanted three Astons and two Lagondas at Le Mans; it was too much as the chapter of retirements in the 1954 season showed. Best results were a Jaguar-swamping 1, 2, 3 at Silverstone and a third at Buenos Aires. At Le Mans, two new coupé bodies proved aerodynamically unstable and both crashed at the White House, another broke a stub axle after a visit to the sand while the original team car DB3S/1 was fitted with a supercharger to give 240bhp against the 225bhp that the twin-plug head cars were now producing; it eventually retired with gasket failure after 20 hours when placed sixth.

The RB6 engine developed for the DBR1 used a new block under the old DB3S head with 60° valve angle; with dry sump lubrication the 3-litre produced up to 250bhp in this form.

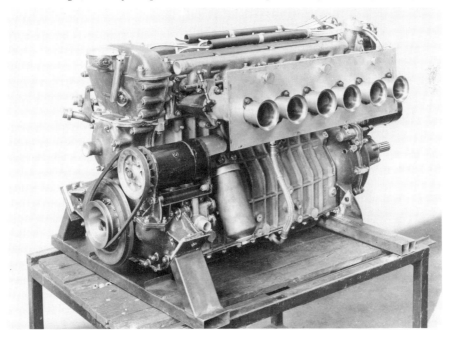

Major departure from the twin-tube theme was this space frame chassis designed for the DBR1, viewed from the rear.

Lessons learnt and the 1954/5 winter was spent in developing the DB3S to its highest potential, continuing with the twin-plug heads but with new rods, crankcase and crankshaft and, later, a camshaft revision to bring the output to 240bhp. Disc brakes were added and the spiral bevel from the Lagonda's final drive was transferred to the DB3S.

The 1955 cars were certainly an improvement with victory in just about every home-based event with an impressive 1, 2, 3, 4 at the British GP supporting race at Aintree. Internationally though, it was Mercedes' year with the 300SLR; although Aston Martin clocked a second place at Le Mans following the post-accident SLR retirement, the only other confrontation came at Dundrod for the TT. Here Collins did get among the SLRs, but the engine wilted under the strain and a fourth behind the Mercedes for Walker/Parnell was the best that could be expected.

During the year, with Wyer as Technical Director, the company started work on the DB4 and a new racing engine, the RB6. This, and

Opening out the valve angle to 95° allowed bigger valves for the RB6 engine. Note the twin plug heads.

the car that it was to power, the DBR1, was put in the care of Ted Cutting. The RB6 was a light alloy unit with seven conventional main bearings, cross-bolted, new crankshaft and connecting rods, but designed to fit under the twin-plug LB6 head. The DBR1 followed the thinking that went into the revised Lagonda chassis, DP166; it used a space frame, retaining trailing arm front suspension, but the de Dion axle was now restrained by a Watt linkage laterally, while the gearbox moved to a transaxle in unit with the final drive, a David Brown 5-speed system.

With winter work devoted to this new car for 1956, little more development was carried out on the DB3S, although it was to be the mainstay. Its victories came in national events, but internationally it was Ferrari who was ahead at Rouen and Jaguar at Le Mans. The French 24-hour race saw the debut of the DBR1 in 2½-litre form, as the organisers had reduced the allowed capacity for prototypes, although such production cars as Jaguar D and DB3S were unrestricted. In the

Tony Brooks/Noel Cunningham-Reid won Nurburgring 1957. Here Moss, who was to win the next two years for Aston, talks to Reg Parnell. David Brown and John Wyer, after his Maserati had lost a wheel.

event Moss/Collins finished second in a DB3S and the DBR1, running lean to conserve fuel, ran its bearings after 20 hours when placed seventh.

For 1957 race team management was placed under Reg Parnell and it was essentially a DBR1 year with mixed success, but a victory at Nurburgring was one highlight followed by two victories at Spa. For the second Brooks' winning car had the new 95° included valve angle head and 252bhp against the 240bhp with the old 60° LB6 derivative.

There was a new car on the stocks too. Tadek Marek had been designing the DB4 engine of 3670cc, an all-aluminium engine capable of 280bhp. The old Lagondas had been sold with their original DP115 chassis, so the space frame DP166 was against the wall, just waiting for such an opportunity as to provide a trial run for the DB4 unit. With a new DBR1-like body, this became the DBR2. Its first outing was at Le Mans where it was entrusted to the Whitehead brothers, as it was felt too new for the works' team. In fact, the DBR1s had transaxle problems, while the DBR2 with a normal gearbox arrangement pumped all the oil out of that, so Le Mans '57 saw no works finisher, although a private French DB3S took eleventh.

For 1958 the International authorities had decreed that sports cars were to be reduced to 3-litres, and suddenly the Aston team had the

The DBR2 used the second Lagonda chassis DP166 with the prototype DB4 engine and was very successful on the British circuits.

41

With the DB4 engine up to 3910cc for 1958, Brooks (67) and Salvadori chase Masten Gregory's Lister-Jaguar. The Lister won from Salvadori and Brooks had a final drive failure.

While single-seater thoughts had loomed before, the first Aston single-seater was this narrowed DB3S which Reg Parnell took to New Zealand in January 1956 without success.

An early test session for the DBR4 at Goodwood in early 1959; unfortunately the car had missed the 1958 season when it might have stood a fair chance.

ideal car. Jaguar were not able to do well with a reduced version of their 3.8-litre, so the main opposition was to be Ferrari. At home though, capacity was unlimited so the DBR2 became the flagship with only Lister-Jaguars to contend with.

During this sports car activity, Aston had also found time to build a GP car, using a smaller version of the DBR1 chassis as the DBR4; a single DBR3 raced once in 1958 using wishbone front suspension and a 3-litre version of the DB4, but the car was converted to a standard DBR1 thereafter.

Single seater thoughts had reared before and one was nearly built for the 2-litre 1952/3 GP period with a reduced LB6, but Eberhorst rejected it. They tried again for the 2½-litre formula due to start in 1954 with a reduced width DB3S, but again Eberhorst was against using a non-purpose built car in Grands Prix. However the new DBR4 could have been ready to make a reasonable impression in 1958 while front-engined cars still led, but the decision was taken to concentrate on the sports cars, leaving the DBR4 to moulder for another year.

Despite the concentration of effort, 1958 was not a good year, marred by troubles with the transaxle on the DBR1. Sebring saw no result for two cars, Moss' singleton run at the Targa Florio saw the fastest car out with gearbox failure, Le Mans saw a crash, a gearbox failure and a blown engine (salvaged by the Whitehead's second place in the DB3S which had taken the same spot three years earlier) but Nurburgring's victory by Moss and a 1, 2, 3 in a truncated TT showed the promise was still there. The DBR2 fared better with a couple of victories but a defeat by Lister-Jaguar at Spa.

For 1959 some effort was to be expended on the DBR4 which had a best race result of second place by Salvadori in the Daily Express Formula One race, but the best GP result was a sixth place at both the British and Portuguese GPs with Salvadori driving. Basically, the RB6 was not up to the extra revs demanded in 2½-litre GP form. In 3-litre sports form, though, the RB6 developed 240-250bhp at 6000rpm; the 2½-litre was being asked to produce the same at 7500rpm and lubrication suffered until the crank oilways were improved.

1959 was to be the year that David Brown was going to win Le Mans; nothing else was supposed to matter as far as the DBR1 was concerned. However, the Sebring organisers prevailed upon Astons to send one car, but Salvadori/Shelby retired after a mere 32 laps through inadequate preparation. The non-championship Silverstone race saw Moss second to a Lister-Jaguar while the DB4GT prototype won the GT race. It was Moss who persuaded Wyer to send a single DBR1 to Nurburgring, which he won with Jack Fairman, and then finally came Le Mans.

Much work had been expended on the transmission and, after the Le Mans test week-end, wind-tunnel tests had shown the desirability of raising the rear deck to catch the air-flow as it came over the screen top. The team went with three cars, Moss/Fairman in DBR1/3 using a four-bearing version of the RB6 for an extra 15bhp, Salvadori/Shelby in DBR1/2 and Trintignant/Frere in DBR1/4. Moss was to press the Ferraris in the opening stages, which he did to such an extent that two were out with blown cylinder head gaskets not long after Moss' engine itself had given up. Salvadori/Shelby then took the lead, only to lose it during the night to the Gendebien/Hill Ferrari, but the heat of the Sunday mid-day sun saw that too retire with overheating, and it was an

Start of Le Mans 1959 with Moss leading the pack away with intent to blow up the Ferraris, which he achieved. D-type, Tojeiro and a works Costin-Lister follow.

Nearing the end of the gruelling 24-hour race is the 1959 winning car with Carroll Shelby still at the helm talking to Eric Hind.

Moments before the great fire that nearly destroyed Aston's chances of clinching the 1959 sports car championship. John King (nearest) and Jim Potton change wheels while Brian Clayton tries to open the filler cap; petrol is already coming from the refuelling pipe.

Twenty-two years on and the car that won at both Le Mans and Goodwood is being driven again by Roy Salvadori with Jack Fairman in the passenger seat on the occasion of the Nimrod launch.

Motor Show 1959 and Sir David Brown stands proudly alongside the Le Mans/ Goodwood winning car.

First outing for the DBR5 with Maserati transaxle and front curving de Dion tube was at Silverstone 1960 where Trintignant came tenth.

For 1960 an 80° head was designed for the DBR4/5 with reserved ports. John King stands by the single cylinder test engine.

Aston 1, 2 run to the finish – Salvadori/Shelby to the fore. At last, David Brown had achieved his personal goal.

It so happened that in 1959 there were very few rounds of the Sports Car championship and, with two victories under its belt, Aston Martin was leading with only the Goodwood TT to go; Ferrari and Porsche were also in with a chance. Parnell teamed Moss/Salvadori, Shelby/Fairman and Frere/Trintignant; Moss led from the start backed by Salvadori, but the car caught fire at its second pit stop, retiring the entry and rendering that pit useless for further work; the privateer Whiteheads in their DBR1/5 retired and lent their pit to the works; Moss replaced Fairman in the DBR1/2 and went on to win.

Aston Martin not only won Le Mans but also the World Sports Car Championship. On top of the world, they decided to retire from sports car racing, but to try again with the now outdated Grand Prix car. Suffice to say that, even with independent rear suspension in DBR5 form, Maserati transaxle and reversed port 80° valve angle head, it never shone and would be best forgotten had the DBR4 not sub-sequently proved very effective in Historic racing. In fact Astons were all set to go one stage further with the DBR4 and had borrowed a mid-engined gearbox from Maserati; they removed the rear chassis frame of DBR4/2 in preparation for installing the Maserati gearbox with the mid-mounted RB6/250 but the project was closed early in 1961 when the company withdrew from racing. By then the 1½-litre Formula One had come into being for which Aston had no power unit, but a number of racing teams had rebelled and tried to get a 3-litre Intercontinental formula going. This petered out in everywhere but Australia where Lex Davison and Bob Stilwell were to campaign the DBR4s with fair success as privateers.

Chapter Four

Trendsetter GT

While all the racing described in the previous chapter had been going on, John Wyer was also supervising the birth of the DB4 which was to transcend the now ageing DB2/4. In 1954 Tadek Marek was brought in from Austins as Engine Designer; an expatriate Pole who had fought alongside Britain in the Second World War, Marek initially worked on the update of the LB6 and then in 1955 started on the DB4 unit. Following the failure of the Lagonda V-12 and a rejection of the V-8, this was to be a six-cylinder. Wyer had asked for a 3-litre which could be stretched to 3.5-litres; Marek in turn requested that he should design the engine in cast-iron which he knew, and that it should not be used for racing.

None of that went according to plan. Marek designed the engine at 3670cc at 92×92mm with twin overhead camshafts and seven main bearings. Then, in late 1955, it was found impossible to get the block cast in iron and only an aluminium foundry could take it on; thus the DB4 engine became an all-aluminium unit and therefore eminently suitable for racing – it did well in the DBR2 at 3670cc, was then taken up to 4-litres and finally nearly 4.2-litres, with 349bhp at 6000rpm. It was an engine of classical design with removeable wet liners and wet sump lubrication; the crankshaft was held in conventional bearing caps. With twin SU carburetters it produced 263bhp (gross) at 5500rpm on an 8.2:1 compression ratio, 240bhp (nett) or a real 220bhp in 1958.

When John Wyer became General Manager he appointed Harold Beach as Chief Engineer in 1956. It had already been Beach's task to start work on the DB2/4 replacement in 1954; he used a perimeter frame with wishbone front suspension and a de Dion axle; the prototype used a 3-litre LB6 engine and covered many miles in test body trim.

Wyer wanted the styling to come from Touring of Milan who had earlier rebodied two DB2/4 Mk. IIs with very pretty open Superleggera bodywork – the principle being one of laying aluminium panels onto a lattice of small diameter tubes which Touring had perfected on sports-racing Alfa Romeos and BMWs before the war. When Harold Beach took his prototype over to Milan, Touring then insisted on a platform chassis to give them a basis on which to create their superstructure. Beach accepted the theory and rapidly revised the whole chassis, but retained his wishbones and de Dion suspension.

Finally in July 1957 the first prototype was finished with the Marek engine, Touring bodywork and the new chassis. It was instantly accepted although, by the time the production was finalised, the rear suspension had reverted to a live axle located by four trailing links and a Watt linkage.

The virtue of a de Dion is that it considerably diminishes the inter-effect of one wheel hitting a bump disturbing the wheel at the opposite

Touring Superleggera executed a striking design on a pair of DB2/4 Mk. IIs in 1956. This is the first one at the Turin Show that year and was the start of the Aston-Touring relationship.

Harold Beach stands alongside the prototype DB4 chassis before it went to Milan for its Touring bodywork.

Close up of the clean simple DB4 platform chassis; this was built at Huddersfield and the superstructure added at Newport Pagnell.

end of the axle; if you hit one end of a light beam supporting two heavy weights, the beam will pivot about the opposite weight – its centre of percussion; hit a pencil, or some homogeneous bar, and it will pivot inboard of the far end exerting an opposite moment at the far end; put a heavy lump like a final drive unit in the middle of a beam, the percussion centre moves even further inboard of the far wheel and exerts a greater down force on it, which will in turn lift the chassis and start a sideways tramp which has to be cured by damping. Unfortunately it was no such technical discussion which ruled out the de Dion here; it was the simple fact that the David Brown gearbox was too noisy to be absorbed with a chassis mounted differential casing.

But by the time the launch came at the beginning of October 1958 there were only two cars built, one demonstrator and one Show car. At that time, bodywork and final assembly were carried out at Newport Pagnell and chassis were built in Huddersfield, but Feltham was still the HQ with design, racing and service. Following the move of the mechanical side of production, as opposed to coachbuilding, to Newport Pagnell, the new centre was faced with a clash of trade unions,

First production DB4, 101/R shows how much luggage can be packed with a little care.

Early DB4s had the front-hinged bonnet shown here on chassis 137 fitted with a sunshine roof.

the National Union of Vehicle Builders, which had previously held sway, and the Amalgamated Union of Engineering Workers employed for the mechanical production. Having survived together for a couple of years they chose the launch of the new, and expensive, DB4 to cause disruption. For a small company which was not at that time making profits it was nearly disastrous; the Brown philosophy was that while the company was racing any loss could be set against the advertising benefit to the David Brown Group. Without such justifiable loss absorption, profit became highly desirable.

Eventually resolved by an agreement over the time required for the various assembly operations, the dispute actually gave the engineering division more time to develop the DB4 which had been rushed into announcement before it was really ready.

Regardless of what was to come, the DB4 had an enthusiastic reception. *Autosport's* comment was one of many on the same theme: *'Years of racing experience have gone into this wonderful vehicle and, as a result, it is the safest and fastest saloon in the world. It is another British achievement that will make the Italians and the Germans think very hard'*. *Motor's* top speed came out at a shade under 140mph, *Autocar's* a shade over; their average for the 0-100mph figure came out at 20.9 seconds, making the claimed 0-100-0 in under 30 seconds easy to achieve. Both these tests were carried out in the autumn of 1960, almost two years after the announcement and the cars had the optional oil cooler, the absence of which had caused heart searching earlier that year.

With the dispute and the fact that the cars which had been sold were mostly in Britain, there had been little experience of the prolonged high speeds attainable in Germany and Italy. Bearing failures resulted from high oil temperatures, so oil coolers became options and by the time the Series 2 came in 1960 the sump capacity had also been enlarged. Meanwhile, the short wheelbase DB4GT had been introduced with triple Webers and 272bhp in October 1959, with its Zagato bodied version arriving in October 1960 – covered in the next chapter.

On the production scene, the last of the 3-litre Lagondas had been

Factory line-up of DB4s on the right and DB4GTs awaiting fitment of their mechanical components and trim.

made in 1957 and David Brown wanted its replacement to emerge from a lengthened DB4, with 16 inches added to the wheelbase and 18½ inches to the overall length. It also featured the first use of the DB4 engine stretched to 4-litres with a 4mm overbore, and produced 236bhp on a pair of twin-choke Solex carburetters; the de Dion axle was a prelude to that for the DBS.

It was not a success and only 55 were sold between 1961 and 1964, but it kept the Lagonda name alive for a little longer before the next ten-year gap. My own driving experience of one of the Rapides was not entirely representative as the car had actually been used for racing and had clocked over 140mph at Jabekke, but it was a spacious and very comfortable four-seater with pleasantly sporting handling. In the

The Lagonda Rapide was announced in 1961 and saw the first use of the 4-litre version of the DB4 engine and De Dion rear axle.

factory it wasn't very popular as it caused considerable production problems. John Wyer accepted it only reluctantly as it hived off half his engineers at a time when the DB4 was in need of further refinement and they could sell all they could make anyway. Wyer admits that this involvement with an unwanted off-spring was a major contribution to his decision to leave Aston Martin, which he did at the end of 1963.

At this time, the DB4 went through a number of improvements, each sufficient to justify a different series number and something to talk about at each Motor Show. After a year and 249 cars the Series 2 offered an overdrive option, increased sump capacity, front-hinged bonnet. Some 350 of these were produced before minor body changes were shown in the spring of 1961. Only half a year on and 164 cars later

January 1960 saw the introduction of the Series 2 with front-hinged bonnet, bigger sump and better front brakes.

Classic view of the DB4 with its graceful fast-back styling giving a raring-to-go impression.

First shown in 1961 the convertible was designed by Harold Beach with the hood mechanism by George Moseley. It was eventually introduced at the end of the Series 4 run.

The Series 5 DB4 came in September 1962 with a little more headroom, GT instruments and 15-inch wheels. Most had the triple SU Vantage engine and some even had the triple Weber GT unit.

In July 1963 the Series 5 DB4 was phased gradually into the DB5 with the 4-litre engine developing 240bhp (282 claimed), ZF 5-speed transmission, fared GT headlights and Girling discs instead of the DB4's Dunlops.

DB5 convertible came in with the DB5 and was presented in suitable fresh air surroundings.

Also offered for the DB5 was this steel hardtop. Note the different rear lights which came in with the DB4 Series 4.

came the Series 4 with bonnet and intake changes, also the option of triple SU 252bhp Vantage, or triple Weber 272bhp GT states of tune and the availability of the first drophead coupé on the DB4 chassis.

A year later after 230 cars, came the Series 5 with three inches added to the overall length to improve interior space; most of these cars were fitted with the Vantage engine and cowled headlamps from the DB4GT. Thus by 1963 the DB4 had reached its definitive stage, a fast and comfortable tourer with a lot more refinement than the early cars. Despite that, the price of the standard DB4 had only increased by £10 from the £3980 announcement, with the Vantage GT versions only £180 extra.

Then in the autumn of 1963 came what was arguably the nicest of the Marek six-cylinder cars, the DB5 in production for just two years and 1025 cars, including 125 dropheads and a dozen estate cars. That was a rate of production that had doubled over previous years and which the DB6 wasn't to match.

The DB5 was essentially the Series 5 DB4 fitted with the 4-litre engine seen in the Rapide with the bore now 4mm larger than the 92mm stroke. It used the Vantage's triple SUs and virtually the same compression ratio (8.9 against 9.0) to offer a claimed 282bhp at 5500rpm – 242bhp was the test-bed norm. To get more Avon rubber on the road the wheels were reduced to 15-inch to take 6.70-15 Turbospeed tyres against the original DB4's 6.00-16. It was 1¾cwt heavier than the DB4, but the extra power added 5mph to the maximum speed at 145mph (for *Motor*) and improved the 0- 100mph acceleration time from 20.1 to 16.9 seconds, doubtless also assisted by the ZF 5-speed gearbox which gradually replaced the old David Brown 4-speed plus overdrive. It was certainly a fast car, but still with excellent roadholding for its day; the handling, on cross-ply tyres still, was better than that of the all-independent Jaguar E-type, but the ride was certainly inferior. Brakes, which were by now Girling instead of Dunlop discs, were completely fade free and gave a 1g stop with only 75lb pedal pressure. Despite the high performance it was still reasonably economical, able to return 17½mpg even with road testers hard at work, with nearly 20mpg possible even at 90mph.

Not long after the launch date the David Brown HQ decided that Feltham was too far from Newport Pagnell, and with the end of racing

A dozen shooting brake DB5s were made by Harold Radford, an elegant solution for those requiring high-speed dog-parks.

Most famous of all the DB5s was James Bond's transport in Goldfinger. On the occasion of the film's launch in Philadelphia, the Chief of Police shows machine guns, extendable bumper rams and rotating number plate.

UK publicity shot of the James Bond DB5 shows the car with its proper number, denoting DP216 which started life as a DB4 Series 5 and became the prototype DB5.

all Feltham personnel should move to the production factory. At the time over half the service, engineering and racing staff were expected to make the move but in the end virtually only Harold Beach and Tadek Marek of the design team were to uproot themselves. It would have been a severe setback if they hadn't, as they were both well into the design of a DBS and its V-8 power unit.

The removed engineering HQ still managed to produce the DB6 in the final attempt to make the car into a genuine adult four-seater; to a large extent they succeeded. An extra four inches in the wheelbase allowed more leg and headroom in the back seat, while the rear end featured a Kamm tail which had shown its virtues in the DP212-5 Le Mans cars; the new tail with a slight upward kick halved the aerodynamic lift and increased boot space too. In construction the DB6 lost the Touring heritage with the wheelbase extension and used a fabricated steel superstructure. Other external changes were the front bumpers that were split in the middle to allow a generous air intake for the oil cooler, while the rear ones were also split. Automatic transmission was available as a no-cost option to the ZF 5-speed while power steering, using a ZF hydraulic ram, was also offered and there was a choice between triple SUs at 282bhp or triple Webers at 325bhp or real 240 and 270bhp.

Motor and *Autocar* both tested the same Vantage version clocking 147.6 and 148mph respectively. I was working on *Motor* at the time and we had expected to clear the magic 150mph which an arguably 'tuned' E-type had achieved in 1961, but the car never quite made it, even after it had been back to Astons and we tried again on the M1. That apart, the DB6 was a fine car; it was very fast to 100mph, reached in 15 seconds dead, which was 1.9 seconds faster than the ¾cwt lighter DB5, so there was certainly a useful power increase. It was left to *Autosport* a year later with a different car to record 152mph and satisfy the honour

The DB6 was announced in October 1965 with an extra 3¾in for the wheelbase, split bumpers and the lift reducing rear spoiler as obvious external differences. Two bunnies emphasise that the engine has four litres and twin overhead camshafts.

David Brown had the first DB6 shooting brake built on the seventh DB6; six more were to follow.

The DB6 Volante came in 1966 but this shot was taken for the 1967 Motor Show to emphasise that the DB6 would continue alongside the DBs.

Her Majesty the Queen and HRH the Duke of Edinburgh visited Newport Pagnell on April 4th 1966; here David Brown hands over a scaled down DB5 Volante for Prince Andrew.

The DB6 continued until July 1969 when the Mk. II was announced with flared arches to take DBS wheels and optional Brico fuel injection. Some 240 cars were built before the last of the DB4 developments was built in November 1970.

of Newport Pagnell.

The longer wheelbase actually improved the car's handling, the controllability enhanced by the superbly progressive Avon GT cross-plies of the time. We felt the ride was getting a little dated, although the standard Selectaride rear dampers helped, but we still described it as 'A Very Grand Tourer'. The extra power was beginning to tell on the fuel consumption though, as our overall figure was 12.5mpg and the 90mph figure had dropped from 20mpg to 15mpg in fourth or fifth! It was, though, a true family man's sports car, as much fun to drive far and fast as to potter around town; the controls had that masculine feel and the instruments were still a splendid array concentrated in front of the driver.

At the time of the DB6 launch a new name was coined for the drophead, Volante. In fact the early ones were really just DB5s with revised bumpers, followed a year later by the real thing with the DB6 tail and an electric hood mechanism. By now, despite the new model, the developed DB4 was beginning to show its age and the lack of American sales – due to emission problems – led to a stockpile of DB6s. In mid-1967 David Brown (knighted the following year) dramatically slashed £1000 off from £5090 to £4070 with the Volante £500 more. By now, the DBS was launched, but the DB6 was partially revitalised in 1969 with wider wheels and tyres (and associated flared wheel arches) as the Mk. II. Options included air conditioning from DBS experience and the AE Brico electronic fuel injection. This last was sadly some years ahead of its time, having first been shown in 1966; Aston Martin was the first to use it, but it was never really perfected before AE sold the system to Lucas who promptly put it into cold storage – or long term development – while they continued their own PI system, which incidentally Aston had tried on a DB4 back in 1961 and finally rejected two years later. A year later, after four years overlap with the DBS, the last DB6 emerged after some 1750 had been produced in Mk. I, Mk. II and Volante form plus a handful of estate car conversions

In 1958 the DB4 was a trendsetter; 12 years on and vastly refined, the DB6 retired quietly, almost unmourned.

Chapter Five

Racing improves the Breed

While the company had raced their saloons in the early days of the DB2, most of the racing in the 1953-9 period was with purpose-built cars. However, racing was still very much in the Aston Engineering mind with both departments still down at Feltham, and early 1959 saw the building of an experimental short wheelbase version of the DB4-DP199. With five inches taken out of the wheelbase leaving only a platform for luggage, thinner gauge aluminium and generally lighter trimming, the GT weighed some 200lb less than the DB4. With triple 45DCO Webers and 12-plug heads, the production engines produced 267bhp at 6000rpm. Cowled headlights helped the drag factor.

The car first appeared in the GT race at the International Trophy meeting of May 1959. That was the day that gave the DBR4 its best result with Salvadori's second place to Brabham's Cooper. This was the first ever GT race which possibly accounted for the rather motley opposition to Stirling Moss in DP199; he won at a canter from Salvadori in a Coombs 3.4 Jaguar, but a lap at 1 minute 55.8 seconds showed a lot of promise. Salvadori's revenge on Moss came later in the sports car race when his Cooper-Maserati beat the DBR1 into second place. They were versatile in those days, because Salvadori used his 3.4 Jaguar again in the Saloon race and was second again – to Ivor Bueb's similar car this time.

The same DP199 was taken to Le Mans that year driven by the Swiss distributor H. Patthey with J. Calderari; as the 3-litre limit was in being at the time, the car ran with the de-stroked engine that had been used in the DBR3 and, of course, it had to run as a prototype. However, after just over an hour, it retired with a bearing failure but some lessons had been learnt, not least the fact that the short-stroke/

69

long rod version of the DB4 unit was not as good as the old RB6. Thus before the DB4GT was announced to the public at the beginning of October, the prototype had already raced twice. With another 60bhp over the heavier DB4, the new car was fast, recording over 150mph, 0-60mph in 6.4 seconds and 0-100mph in 14.2 seconds; with new Girling brakes it had the chance to reduce the 0-100-0mph time to a mere 20 seconds.

Two views of the DB4GT engine which in production form produced 272bhp at 6000rpm against a claimed 302bhp with the Zagato version perhaps 10bhp higher with a 9.7 against 9.0:1 compression ratio. Jogn Ogier's 1962 Le Mans engine gave 293bhp at 6000rpm.

Over the next three years 75 were to be built and they are still highly coveted; hardly road cars in the town-pottering sense, they are still very quick and somewhat noisy, both inside as a result of the unsilenced Weber carburetters, and outside through nominal silencing – an exhilarating Sunday morning road-burner with all the entertainment of perfectly controllable tail slides on old-fashioned cross-ply Turbospeeds.

While the factory had retired from racing they were not beyond producing special lightweight versions for private owners to campaign. John Ogier with the Essex Racing stable bought a pair labelled 17TVX and 18TVX, with which he challenged the Ferrari 250GT squadron at the 1960 Tourist Trophy using such Aston regulars as Salvadori together with Innes Ireland. The two Astons finished second and third only to Stirling Moss in the Rob Walker Ferrari.

71

Works experimental DB4GT O167R had a lightweight chassis and Zagato spec engine. John Bolster tested it for Autosport in 8:12:61 issue and clocked 152.5mph and 0-60mph in 6.4 seconds.

Standard DB4GT emphasises cowled lights but loss of 5in from wheelbase makes little difference to DB4 lines.

For the 1960 Motor Show Astons had been preparing a new version of the DB4GT with bodywork by the Milanese coachbuilders Zagato. Standard DB4GT chassis were sent out to Milan to be clad by Zagato and the majority were to return to Astons to be completed, although Zagato finished a handful themselves. The first DB4GT had been numbered 101; the first Zagato was to use the last number in the GT series, 200, doubtless to convince the relevant authorities that the requisite 100 had been built in a 12-month to conform with Appendix J, group 3, a dodge comparable to those employed in Maranello at the time – subsequent bodywork changes were allowed provided the suspension mountings were unchanged. In fact the standard Zagatos were very little lighter than the DB4GT, as the homologation tolerance was only 5 per cent. However, this did enable lightweight Zagatos to be built for racing with a further 150lb removed.

The first car had its first outing at the 1961 Goodwood Easter Monday meeting where Stirling Moss took a thus far unsorted car into

Zagato bodywork on O185 emphasises the double bubble effect that Zagato transferred from the roof of Abarth Fiats to the Aston's bonnet shape.

The lowest numbered Zagato O176 was almost the last to be built as the first car started at O200. This is the very original low mileage car formerly owned by Victor Gauntlett.

Wide angle lens heightens the unpleasant effect of adding a rear bumper to protect the Zagato's thin panelling. The boot is full of 30-gallon fuel tank and spare wheel.

third place behind a 250GT and 17TVX. The lightweight Zagatos were being prepared for John Ogier to take to Le Mans – the famous 1 VEV and 2 VEV, 182 and 183 respectively. Both cars were afflicted with gasket trouble after 2½ hours, but Kerguen in the left hand drive 180 suffered electrical troubles in the final hour when lying ninth; two DBR1s in private hands fared as unsuccessfully.

Lex Davison's victory over Jack Sears' Coombs E-type at Aintree in 2 VEV was some recompense. Came the TT and the Ogier team took on the Ferraris, but couldn't beat Moss and Parkes in the fastest of Maranello; they were rewarded with third, fourth and fifth plus the team prize for 1 VEV, 2 VEV and faithful 17TVX.

A further pair of lightweight Zagatos labelled MP 209 came out in 1962 for privateers David Skailes and Frenchman Kerguen who was to return again to Le Mans that year, only to suffer transmission failure after 11½ hours. These had an entirely special drilled box girder chassis under their otherwise standard looking bodywork.

DP stood for Design Project applied initially to small and large

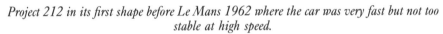

Project 212 in its first shape before Le Mans 1962 where the car was very fast but not too stable at high speed.

projects alike. Around the end of the 'fifties the small projects were hived off into four-figure numbers leaving sub-1000 numbers to major exercises. By 1961 this was as confusing inside the factory as outside to the historian, so the low number DPs became Master Projects from MP207 onwards with no retrospective renumbering, but at least they knew where they were going at the time! Thus it is correct to refer to the Project cars but not to DP212, by then it was MP212.

As a postscript to the disorderly chassis numbering of the series, the first number 176 went to a car built in 1962 at which point the numbering met the rising numbers of DB4GTs. Although the Aston banner was being flown quite successfully by the privateers on both sides of the Atlantic, dealers generally wanted the works to make a return to Le Mans in particular; thus MP 212 was born as much a development tool as an outright racer.

Le Mans that year was allowing a 4-litre GT prototype category, so the GT engine was increased to 4-litres and given 50 DCO Webers to produce 327bhp. The car itself was a lightened 4GT chassis but with de Dion rear suspension, clothed in low drag potential four-seater bodywork, a prototype within the spirit of the law. It was very fast and Graham Hill actually led the 24-hour race at the end of the first lap and was second to the winning prototype Ferrari 330P at the end of the first hour, but electrical delays dropped it down the field and a broken oil line stopped it altogether after five hours.

In September 1962, MP212 was taken to Silverstone for Ritchie Ginther to test various improvements under the eye of Ted Cutting. On the sixth they established a base time of 1 minute 53 seconds. In an effort to combat the high speed tail lift, they had a flat tail and spoiler grafted on; Ginther reduced the time to 1 minute 49 seconds. Next the front roll centre was raised from a low 1-inch to a still low 1¾-inch and bigger tyres were fitted; the time came down to 1 minute 46 seconds. In effect they had improved the rear grip but needed to add more understeer. They returned again on the tenth with a stiffer de Dion tube and a lowered rear roll centre to get the roll axis more nearly horizontal and started straight away at 1 minute 46 seconds on a slightly damp track. Slackening the front anti-roll bar improved this still further to 1 minute 44.8 seconds.

November's report stated that the lessons were to be transferred to the new cars MP214 and 215. The missing number – MP213 – was that used for the new V-8 which they hoped to use in MP215 during 1964. Two MP214s were to be nominal homologated GT cars and took numbers 194 and 195 from the GT series; in fact the chassis was very similar to that developed for the lightweight Zagatos but the suspension was 4GT, while the engine was 4GT bored out 1mm and equipped with 50DCO Webers to give 317bhp – these cars were labelled MP214. MP215 was openly special with an even lighter boxed girder with a cruciform centre section, dry sump 4-litre engine giving 323bhp, wishbone independent rear suspension and the David Brown 5-speed transaxle from the DBR1. Bodies on all three cars followed the MP212 theme but improved stability with a sharply cut-off Kamm tail.

The MP214 cars' use of the chassis that had been developed for the lightweight Zagatos obviously helped their rapid development. They were, however, hardly within the spirit of the rules of the day, but the

This shot of Innes Ireland, about to finish sixth overall and second GT behind Sears'
Ferrari GTO in the 1963 Guards Trophy, shows MP214 with the tail modifications that
stabilised the bodyshape for Le Mans 1963.

The interior of Project 215 shows the well drilled box section chassis braced by a cruciform; bodywork was certainly superleggera.

Project 215 undergoing testing at Silverstone.

Off to Le Mans tet week end in April 1963 with 212 on top of the two 214s.

three cars went to Le Mans to compete in GT and GT prototype categories.

Project 215 went out after three hours with transmission failure without starring, while both 214s went out with detached piston crowns – a function of using cast rather than forged pistons – McLaren/Ireland after five hours having reached sixth, and Kimberley/Schlesser after 10 hours when lying third. The cars were certainly fast, as Ireland was the first man to achieve 300kph down the Mulsanne straight but the development time for the team wasn't long enough – that was the first race that season. MP215 lost a chance of winning a race at Rheims when Schlesser missed gear changes and bent valves, but the two MP214s were entered for the Tourist Trophy. There the scrutineers decided that the wheel rims didn't conform to the homologation papers so the cars ran on reduced track and Ireland could only muster seventh while combating massive oversteer.

The MP214s had their revenge at Monza for a 3-hour race when Salvadori beat Mike Parkes in a Ferrari 250GTO by a few car lengths with Bianchi third in the second MP214. As a French dessert course the cars then finished 1, 2 at Montlhery. At the end of the season John Wyer left to join the Ford GT40 programme, and, although he had long been general manager, that marked the end of Aston Martin racing as an entity; henceforth Aston was to supply engines but not complete cars for International racing.

As a postscript, MP212 and the two 214s were acquired by Dawnay Racing and continued to compete in International racing, albeit without major success. The senior partner in Dawnay Racing was to become Viscount Downe, who once again took Aston Martin back to the tracks with his privately entered Aston Nimrod in 1982/3/4.

Chapter Six

More Space Less Speed

Following the autumn 1965 launch of the DB6, Aston production stepped up to 11 cars a week, building up to the remarkable figure of 18 by June 1966. It must be borne in mind by those familiar with the Newport Pagnell factory that the sheet metal platform of the chassis was still being built in Huddersfield, so a lot more space was available for panel beating and assembly than these facilities now use. Then came Harold Wilson's economy measures in late July. They included a 10 per cent rise in purchase tax and excise duties, and hire purchase restrictions that increased the required deposit to 40 per cent and cut the pay-back period from three to two years. Thus petrol went up from the now laughably low 5s (25p) per gallon to 5s.4d (26.7p) and the DB6 increased from £4998 to £5084 against a basic price of £4135. While none of this seems particularly catastrophic in today's terms, the general climate of the time was discouraging towards spending, and a DB6 Vantage returned less than 14mpg when driven hard.

The effect on Aston Martin was initially out of all proportion, until people had adjusted. Orders were cut back, so production was reduced rapidly through a three-day week to ten cars a week, and there were soon upwards of 130 DB6s cluttering the available space and more. It wasn't until the following year that David Brown slashed the price by £1000, by which time some confidence had returned and the car park began to empty – not until the second year of the DB6 Mk. II (1970) did the price transcend the 1966 level.

Prior to this Aston Martin had been directing thoughts towards a new four-seater to take the still developing V-8 once the DB6 was under way. In fact a year before the DB6 was launched, Touring had already been briefed to start design work on MP220. In October 1964, Aston engineers conducted a long Continental trip in DP200, registered 4 YMC. This had started as a sort of DB4 but was fitted with the 4-litre Weber carburetted engine giving 263bhp at 5800rpm, a ZF 5-speed gearbox, a de Dion rear axle and the first long wheelbase frame. A visit to Webers eliminated a flat-spot, but time was taken to view Touring's preliminary work on ¹⁄₁₀th scale drawings of MP220. MP216 had been the ex DB4 series prototype DB5, MP217 was a development DB5 and MP219 had been a prototype DB6. However that 3492-mile Continental trip showed 15.3mpg and 3150mpg of oil. Somewhat unbelievably the report writer also produced flying kilometre times of 14.2 and 14.0 seconds or 158.5mph at 6200rpm and 160.5 at 6275rpm; the gradient and wind speed weren't mentioned. Sadly by this time Touring was in financial difficulties. It is worth looking back at the Milanese company which had had such an important influence on Aston history.

Carrozzeria Touring was founded in 1926 by Felice Bianchi Anderloni and Gaetano Ponzoni. Anderloni had studied law but went to work for Isotta Fraschini in 1904; before and after that time his three

Touring's MP220 model from drawing dated 11:2:68. While this has the virtue of four seats, the reasons for lack of interest in this bland square-rigged shape are evident.

sisters married into the Isotta and Fraschini families, but that didn't help his career particularly. He worked as an engineer and did a certain amount of racing, where he performed well in National events. The Great War saw him in the army acting as liaison officer for the military production of Isotta Fraschini. After the war the families had lost control of Isotta Fraschini and Anderloni went to work for the Peugeot Italiano offshoot of the controlling company.

Ponzoni was nine years younger and had also trained as a lawyer but had gone into banking. In 1925 Anderloni took the majority shareholding in Carrozzeria Falco when selling Peugeots had finally palled; he persuaded his family friend Ponzoni to join him in the new project. Until then it had been run by Vittorio Ascari, brother of Alfa Romeo driver, Antonio. The combination of the Alfa Romeo relationship and Anderloni's earlier association with Isotta Fraschini ensured a good start for the new company.

Taking over the rights of Weymann coachbuilding for that area of northern Italy heralded and underlined Anderloni's perpetual quest for lightness. Weymann's theme was to accept that wooden body frames were not built to strengthen flexible steel chassis; his body frames were designed to flex, which precluded aluminium panels, so the outer covering was in horsehair padded fabric. It was a successful formula for the late twenties.

Touring used the Weymann system into the thirties, building pure Weymann saloons as well as hybrids – aluminium panels below the waistline – on a variety of Italian cars. Body styles were striking whether saloon, sports tourer or out-and-out sports car. Developing the Weymann principle into more modern and more tightly curved shapes meant a return to aluminium but wood was too heavy. The Superleggera system was evolved in 1937 – a lattice of thin-section steel tubes welded together to give the basic body outline. This was welded to the steel chasis, adding deliberately to its rigidity; panel beaten shapes were attached at relatively few points and wrapped round the body tubes where possible. Advertising pictures of the time showed two women holding a complete body frame; it was strong and very light. Thus the system inevitably found rapid favour with the racing fraternity – Lancia, Alfa Romeo and, in 1939, BMW. The 1940 Mille Miglia (or Brescia GP) was full of Touring bodywork on these three marques, added to which was the body for the first Ferrari – the 815, called an AAC as Ferrari's name was still Alfa Romeo property at the time.

Wartime saw Touring in the aero industry while Britain's erstwhile post-war car designers were busy assessing the remarkable performance of the 2-litre BMWs in winning that 1940 race on the 109-mile Brescia triangle against much larger engined cars.

Post-war the Aldingtons, who ran Frazer Nash and had imported BMWs before the war were also associated with Bristol's emergence as car manufacturers; it was small wonder that they continued their pre-war links with BMW, using engine and chassis from 328 and 326. While the Bristol 400 was essentially a revived BMW 327, the new 401 had its aerodynamic shape mounted on a Touring Superleggera body frame; Bristol took out a licence. Meanwhile Ferrari and Alfa Romeo continued to use Touring bodywork for touring and sports bodywork. The first barchetta 166 Ferraris and some of the mid-fifties Testa Rossas, as well as the famous Disco Volante Alfa, were all the work of the Milanese bodybuilders, for whom Anderloni's son was now the technical mainspring following his father's death in 1948. Came the tie-up with Aston Martin for the DB4, following the 1956 Superleggera DB2/4s and that was the most important contract at the time for Touring. Maserati too joined the Touring fold; when Rootes asked them to produce the second generation Alpine in late 1961, Touring had outgrown its original premises. Just under 300 cars a year in the mid-fifties had grown to just under 3000 by 1960.

Coupled with the roseate hue of Italy's entry into the EEC, the time seemed ripe for a bigger home. But that move coincided with an 8-month period of industrial unrest among Italy's metal workers; meanwhile Rootes were getting into financial trouble and cancelled contracts to produce the Super Minx and the Sunbeam Venezia. That was the beginning of the end for Touring; even the birth of Lamborghini was not enough, and, in February 1965, the receiver was called in, despite desperate attempts to head off the evil day with cut-backs. In fact production was to continue until January 1967, but much was happening at Aston Martin too.

MP220 was thus a four-seater Aston on Touring's drawing boards back in Autumn of 1964. Touring's receivership in February 1965 must have caused doubts which took some time to dispel at Aston.

Little happened at either Milan or Newport Pagnell on MP220 during 1965 other than a few calculations on the required shapes for a high speed 4-seater. Aerodynamically the DB4 series had been good for its day; DB4 and DB5 had drag factors of 0.377, the short DB4GT slipped to 0.396 while the longer DB6 with spoiler had improved to 0.364. Arguably a prototype for the high-speed 4-seater, MP212 was best with 0.356. Given the overall drag of the DB4, with some 350bhp available from the V-8 when it came, MP220 was reckoned to be potentially capable of around 180mph.

With the DB6 well received but acknowledged to be ageing as a development of the rounded style of the 1958 DB4, thoughts had moved ahead. The DB6 would take the company through the following show, perhaps with a Volante version; a new fast two-seater would appear in 1967 capable of taking the V-8 in 1968, when the four-seater would also appear complete with V-8. Touring was approached again in January 1966 by the new Engineering Director, Dudley Gershon, to style the two seater based on a pair of prototype chassis that Astons had built up. These used a similar front end to that of the DB6 but the engine had been moved back some 10 inches, getting it behind a cross member to allow it to be lower; presumably this allowed for the V-8 to fit in front of the bulkhead and not to interfere with steering lock, but the longer six cylinder found its last two cylinders under the scuttle. Additionally the rear suspension had been revised to incorporate a de Dion tube – Harold Beach's influence at last gaining expression.

Touring produced their sketches in April and David Brown chose the definitive form. It followed the lines of the Touring-bodied Lamborghini 350GT of 1964 with adjustments to the lighting area and a spoiler lip grafted onto the tail. Then came the Wilson bombshell and orders were immediately cut back for the DB6; a new model was needed for the Motor Show. Such was Touring's state at the time that they agreed to the almost impossible schedule of advancing their completion date by a year. A left hand drive car was completed in time, just, to be joined on the show stand by the DB6 Volante.

Meanwhile some work had been directed towards updating the DB6 with a revised front end, longer and lower. This exercise was completed but it was considered unviable in that it would need widening for the V-8 a year or two later. Earlier that year Harold Beach had interviewed a

Aston Martin

In contrast to MP220, MP226, Touring's 2-seater DBS, was exceptionally good looking; originally styled around the V-8, it had to accept the longer 6-cylinder which had its last two cylinders tucked under the scuttle.

young seat designer from Rover, William Towns. Not that William believed in his ability to be just the ultimate interior designer – he wanted to design a new Aston, but didn't feel he was able to take the parallel opportunity to be Chief Body Engineer which was to be taken by Cyril Honey from Pressed Steel Fisher. Towns was forever sketching exteriors as well as interiors and it was his task to sketch a draft brochure for the DB7 as MP220 might have become; somehow it didn't look as pretty as Towns' own sketches!

Thus when the engineering team discovered that there was a good six months development ahead of them to make the DBS into a sellable proposition, and they couldn't offer delivery dates at the Motor Show, decisions were rapidly taken to abandon Touring's MP220 and 226, and a widened DB6 body shape in the space of little more than a week. Towns's design it was to be, and moreover it would be at the next Motor Show less than a year away – MP227 had to move fast! Producing a new car from stem to stern in that timescale was obviously impossible, so the brief was to follow proven practice and make maximum use of existing components.

The DBS platform shows a marked similarity to that of the DB4 shown in Chapter 4 but it is wider and has a more substantial rear end.

To accommodate the V-8, which was by then almost public knowledge, the chassis had to be wider to clear the twin overhead camshaft per bank layout and provide adequate steering lock. The simplest way to satisfy the width and continuity of components criteria was to widen the existing platform chassis, on the basis that it was known to be amply strong, whereas any totally new chassis design would require proving first. Accordingly the basic DB6 chassis was widened by some 4½ inches, the front wheels moved forward an inch to enable the engine to be lowered behind the front cross member, and finally de Dion rear suspension was added, the latter had been proven in V-8 engined DB5 development cars in which, apart from early cracking of the three-piece tube leading to a one-piece version, it was an instant success.

The car was to measure 15ft overall, two inches shorter than the DB6 which was mostly achieved by reducing rear overhang; mounting the spare wheel vertically at the front of the boot where it was inset into the fuel tank saved three inches. The width grew more than the 4½ inches chassis widening through the adoption of wider wheels and the necessary clearance, so that the DBS finally emerged six feet wide, six inches up on the DB6.

At last a de Dion for a production Aston. Inboard rear brakes took advantage of the Jaguar final drive unit. De Dion tube is located laterally by Watt linkage.

Overall height was to remain at 4ft 4ins but the roof line was to fall away faster than did the DB6; this was achieved by lowering the front seats an inch while the rear seats were dropped 2½ inches, thanks to the use of a de Dion tube behind the axle line, and the chassis-mounted differential didn't require vertical propshaft movement. Rear seat headroom is very similar to that of the DB6, but the greater width creates a more spacious feel. In fact the DBS cross members had to be beefed up to retain the torsional rigidity so the chassis finished up very substantially changed, requiring its own new jigs rather than modified DB6 ones.

At this time the chassis platform was still to be built at David Brown's Huddersfield factory; the fact that many of the original jigs are still in use testifies to the high standards of the tooling that went into the project, despite the unprofitable state of the Aston Martin company at the time.

For the body too, only the shortest possible development time was allowed, which meant that Towns had to produce his final shapes with ease of production in mind, ease too of creating the master shapes right

Front and rear views of the clay model of the DBS shows the Bizzarini-type louvres on the front panel and the intended front-end treatment.

first time. So most of the major characteristics were dictated by finite lines. Thus the roof shape was dictated by occupants' headroom in side view, and the cantrails ran back from the screen top to tail almost parallel all the way. From the cantrail a constant angle of outset dictated where the plane of the waistline must fall, finally delineated by a side view taking wheel arch limits and engine top as points on the waistline curve. The shape between cantrail and waistline followed a fixed radius all along, and below the waistline was a fixed side-section; lifting that section at the rear wheel arch moved the maximum width bulge up by the same amount to give the effect of belling out the arch. A straight base to the door sills carried a simple stainless steel finishing strip. Simple and clinical it may be in hindsight once it is all explained, it was a case of creating your shape and then matching simple 3-D geometry to it; it is the lack of irregularity which has allowed the style to remain classically undated.

The full-size egg-box, a mass of transverse and longitudinal plywood sections slotted together, was then built to create the full-scale shape; the gaps were all filled to make a smooth outline from which glassfibre moulds were taken as masters for aluminium panels to be beaten by hand.

Despite the October 1966 decision, and all the work involved in creating a new shape, plus the added complication of a change in screen rake in June, the first prototype was completed on the night of Monday 17th July, 1967. The next day it was at the Motor Industry test track at Nuneaton (MIRA) for driving and wind-tunnel testing.

To start with it weighed 3538lb empty with 12 gallons of fuel, while the accompanying MP219 DB6 prototype with de Dion was only 45lb lighter; weight distribution showed 48/52 for the DBS against 49¼/50¾ for the DB6. At that time MP227 only had perspex for all its windows. In the wind tunnel, things weren't too impressive. The drag coefficient came out at 0.416 against the DB6 0.364, which, with the 5½ per cent increase in frontal area, showed a probable 270bhp maximum of 144.5mph against the DB6 149.5mph, both being over the power peak by that speed; thus the V-8 would need at least 300bhp just to match the DB6.

Then came the lift figures with the DBS very much worse than the DB6. At an extrapolated 140mph the DBS had 349lb lift at the front end against the DB6 108lb, while the DB6 had a rear downforce of 16lb but the DBS still had 35lb lift. This was enough to change the weight distribution, with driver and passenger, from the already rearward bias of 48/52 to 43/57; this potential instability was apparent to the drivers at speeds over 120mph with the steering getting gradually lighter. However, on the handling circuit the car earned praise for its high cornering force and acceptable unassisted steering weight, while the Girling brakes performed very well.

The spring rates had been carried over from the DB6 but it was felt that the rear rates needed to be in increased due to the extra rearward weight and the car's four-seater potential. Selectaride dampers were retained from the DB6. But in general the car behaved very well considering the first prototype had only been completed the night before.

As WKX 2E, the new car was out on the road during the first half of August for testing under as many varied conditions as possible. It was decided to carry this out away from Newport Pagnell to avoid publicity and David Brown's Sunderland factory was chosen as the base.

One of the early DBSs ready for its first showing to the press; here it is in the R & D building which now houses the Trim Shop.

91

Because the car still had a perspex screen, night driving was precluded in case it rained. Two shifts a day on a 380-400-mile route built up the miles rapidly and Mike Loasby, who had joined the year before, wrote the comments. The handling was rated highly still, but reckoned unsafe at high speed in high side winds; Dunlop SP41 205×15 tyres were fitted. The spring damper set-up worked well but the nominal 1½ inch ground clearance for the silencers on full bump was used up occasionally and a redesigned system was called for. The interior needed to be quieter and there were minor comments on the positions of the various controls. The heating system wasn't functioning due to incorrect assembly. Brake pads had to be changed after the first 3,500 miles so further work was needed there. The total run covered some 10,000 miles in the hands of six drivers, including some journalists being given a preview.

Two trips to MIRA followed in the last week of August and the first week in September, but these were regarded as pretty inconclusive as the results of the first were unrepeatable on the second occasion. The greatest spread came in the drag coefficient which ranged from 0.33 to

Press Day at Blenheim Palace on September 25th, 1967. The AMOC joined in with a massive display of DB models.

92

Press caption for this shot says 'careful development of the body line of the DBS has eliminated the need for an up-lipped spoiler to provide stability at high speeds'. They were still testing stability at this stage!.

Press release montage shows how much luggage you can get into a DBS with its vertically mounted spare wheel.

Engineering DBS before the final underbody shape was arrived at. Bumpers here are split.

0.45 on the first day, but 0.40 to 0.44 on the second; this was deemed to be due to the extreme sensitivity to the angle of attack of the wind – or the position of the car in the tunnel. All that emerged was that an undertray from the front of the lower intake to the rear cross member consistently reduced the lift at the front by as much as 13 per cent. Marek considered it was essential to build a ¼-scale model as the maximum 80mph wind-speed on the full-size tunnel could not fairly be extrapolated. In fact the model was built but as the announcement date was by now very close the car had to be tested on the road with subjective assessment.

In all mechanical aspects the car was performing well, but at the stage of three weeks before launch, a production prototype had not been completed so it was impossible to assess noise and ventilation.

A report concluded that the Research and Development department was not prepared to release the car for production in that form. In fact the car was released to the press during the week beginning

September 25th, 1967, prior to the Motor Show which was to open on October 18th. It was well received and from *Autosport* and *Motor* one discovered that Gregor Grant and Tony Curtis had been on the Scottish trip, the former mentioning that the V-8 was expected to be fitted at a later date.

At the Motor Show Aston somehow managed to find two DBS cars to go onto the stand, a right-hand-drive manual Vantage in Dubonnet red and a left-hand-drive with Borg Warner automatic, triple SUs, power steering and Bosch self-seeking ratio in Amethyst. Alongside were DB6 in Volante and standard forms. While the Aston press-release photo had been of a white car, Autocar's Show number chose to use the prototype that had been in Scotland, complete with Iso Grifo-type louvres in two groups of five running down the side of the car at scuttle level. With such profusion of viewable cars a certain amount of overtime must have been worked, but the R & D department obviously wasn't allowed to get its hands on them.

Disillusioned by the MIRA results, Astons sent the prototype out to Belgium only just before the Motor Show for a series of high speed runs to assess stability, new oil cooling and various tyres. Mike Loasby was again at the wheel and proceeded to measure drag by maximum speed comparisons and lift by subjective feel. Various undertrays were tried, the recessed headlights were fared in and there was even a spoiler air-dam fitted under the front cross member. The more was the gap between front valance and cross member filled in, the lower the drag and the better the feel. Given this panel change, Loasby felt the car was as safe as the DB6 at speed and very much better at high speed cornering.

The original oil cooler was a single unit mounted centrally behind and below the front number plate between quarter bumpers, but this was changed to twin coolers mounted at each side of the radiator with a full width bumper; this dropped oil temperatures at maximum speed from over 85°C to 71°C with an improvement in oil pressure from 55psi to 65psi noted in the fourth gear tests at 5500rpm. As far as the tyres were concerned, Avon was pitted against Firestone and the Dunlop SP41, the latter having a maximum speed rating of 135mph; all felt the same in stability but the radials were judged harder over cobbles, but equally gave a better wear rate. No final decision was taken at that time.

What was also noted was that the bonnet belled out some ⅜-inch suggesting the need for a positive air outlet, the gear lever was too far from the driver and the wipers floated away from the screen at speed. At the end of October a return visit was made to MIRA in which wire-type wiper blades were found to stay on the screen at over 100mph, 8-inch servos gave better braking, the heater wasn't able to deliver cold air and the clutch wasn't up to a 1 in 3 restart.

Most of the items raised by these post-launch tests found their way into the early production cars; it had been too much to hope that the car would be perfect after so rapid a build programme with no time left for development. Inevitably there had to be a series of running changes.

The heating system certainly wasn't the car's strongest point. Basically it followed the DB6 system, running trunking from the front of the car on both sides through the top of each wheel arch and up to blowers each end of the scuttle. Inside the full width plenum chamber

Early DBSs had single control for heating; three knobs on A-post control washer/wipers, Selectaride and panel light rheostat. Mini-skirts were a feature of the late 'sixties.

were diverter valves for volume and foot/screen direction, while the temperature of the twin radiators was controlled by a water valve. In an attempt at total simplification, this was all to be controlled by a single knob; the anti-clockwise 180° went from off to fresh air to maximum fan speed and then a demist position for all flow to screen level; clockwise brought in the water valve gradually with fan speed again putting all to the screen in the final maximum position. Unfortunately the vacuum controlled valve modulators were inclined to stick and the trunking picked up engine heat, more so in the V-8 version to come.

Throwing away the over simplification, Astons then went overboard in manual control for the next stage, with two knobs on the facia to give fan speed and direction while three sliders, by the driver's right knee, gave temperature and choice of air volume to left and right outlets. When air conditioning was fitted, a Frigidaire compressor with condenser in front of the radiator and matrix in the centre of the plenum chamber, an extra knob gave degrees of coolness while the direction knob took on a choice of fresh air, recirculated air, direction of heated air or cold conditioned air only. It was really two separate systems in one.

By 1970 though, they had taken over a proprietary Coolair system with York compressor and all air being conditioned with just three controls, fan speed, temperature and direction. Air was drawn in through the side scuttle vents and, apart from a recent change in control mechanism, this has been in use ever since, although the compressor is now a Sankyo unit. One has to admit that it could be more efficient, but this is hampered by the space available and the fact that it still uses a similar full-width plenum chamber carrying hot and cold matrices.

At the time of its launch the DBS was still fitted with cross-ply tyres; Avon's latest development which replaced the Turbospeed, was the GT of 8.10×15 dimensions on 6-inch rims. Despite that, it was soon apparent that the car needed power steering, particularly for parking speeds. The company had already offered this option on the DB6 and was able to tailor the settings to give the same steering weight on the DBS. Power steering had been very much an American preserve and anyone who fitted it to European cars (Rolls, Jaguar, Mercedes) tended to reproduce American steering weights, which were, and still are, quite unacceptable to anyone with any sporting instinct at all.

The first time I met a good power steering system, that appeared to feel like a direct manual system, was on the NSU Ro80; it was actually difficult to tell that the system had assistance – someone had at least discovered that it wasn't necessary to exaggerate a feature to justify the adoption. The Ro80 used a simple hydraulic ram coupled into the linkage, controlled by a valve block at the base of the column. Aston Martin used the same ZF system mounted neatly on top of the rack.

I remember visiting Newport Pagnell in December 1967; I had hoped to sneak an advance press drive in the recently announced DBS but was quite happy to try a similarly equipped DB6. Astons had set the required effort at about 40 per cent of that for the unassisted system, both at rest and for 10mph manoeuvring. It certainly felt very acceptable although, at the time, I was unconvinced that the damping effect of the hydraulic circuit had not masked the ability to sense the variation in tyre self-aligning torque. Ideally the self-aligning torque curve goes over its peak and lessens the steering effort just before the tyre reaches its peak grip. But Astons, as far as I was concerned, had chosen the right system.

For the occupants it was a traditional Aston; the best of the DB6 was carried over – a classic three-spoke wood rim wheel, behind which, a superb battery of round dials was visible. Pedals sprouted from the floor with a firm confidence-inspiring feel which many called heavy. Electric windows were standard.

One particular feature of the DBS that was to disappear five years later was the use of four $5\frac{3}{4}$-inch headlights which fitted neatly in the shallow ends of the typically Aston shaped grille. The main beam spread and range were good, but the dipped beam with the two outer ones only proved poor by contrast; five years on the design reverted to the current twin 7-inch lights which had been under consideration, but not adopted at the original design stage.

Inevitably with such a rushed programme the production tooling still wasn't complete by the time of the well-received launch at the 1967 Motor Show. However the DBS wasn't replacing the DB6, so the company had a little leeway for delay in responding to the flood of orders for the DBS. It was nearly five months later that production was able to get into full swing and, by the middle of 1968, the DB6 and DBS were being produced in equal numbers, five a week of each.

Second stage of heater development had two central knobs and three sliders. A-post knobs are now on console while T-handle for doors was short-lived.

Although a few journalists had driven prototypes around the launch period, it wasn't until the following July that the company was able to let a few more drive a production car. I went on behalf of *Motor* to Brussels where I was met by the company's PR consultant, Bruce Ells, with a manual DBS; we then drove around Belgian roads before going to Zolder, a circuit I had recently visited to drive the Brabham-Daf F3 car, so I knew it fairly well. I don't normally like thrashing production cars on production tyres around racing circuits, but the combination of the DBS and a nice twisty circuit like Zolder with plenty of interrelated curves and a blind crest approached at speed – no chicane behind the pits then – was a happy association.

The car was certainly slower than the DB6, but 100mph cruising seemed just as effortless and the ride, with a bit of Belgian pave thrown in, was very much better. On the circuit the handling came into its own

Production DBS in 1968 shows the cleanliness of line with sharp sculpture lines and the coke-bottle bell over the rear wheels.

and the large car – larger when you are driving on the wrong side of the road – seemed to shrink around the driver until it appeared to have all the chuckability of a well-sorted Mini. Understeer was the predominant circuit characteristic, but it could be thrown into a corner in an almost oversteer slide and caught when wanted; racing may not have directly improved that particular breed, but it was very much in the minds of the engineers who wanted to design the ultimate in safe, fast machinery. I don't think Bruce Ells was ever quite the same passenger again, particularly as I was taking that hump ever faster with the car getting lighter each time, but I think we were both impressed by the Aston's behaviour – I certainly was.

It was nearly six months later that we had a full road test car which merely served to confirm all my original impressions. We clocked 141.5mph on maximum speed – Belgium again – and the acceleration times gave 0-60mph in 7.1 seconds and 0-100mph in a remarkable 18.0 seconds against the 6.1 and 15.0 of the DB6 with apparently the same engine. The 10 per cent greater weight was perhaps more apparent in

Unusual shot of the DBS shows the bonnet bulge crease ending at the rear of the bonnet and the curved front of the car.

Earls Court 1968 and the DBS is shown alongside the two DB6 models; the DB6 saloon is receiving a final polish.

our overall fuel consumption figures with 10.9mpg for the DBS against an already heavy 12.5 for the DB6. By then the car was on 205×15 Avon radials.

It was interesting to come across the test sheet for that road test engine many years later. By that time Aston had given up quoting power figures, but still gave torque; since that was still the same 290lb ft at 4500rpm which was published for the DB6, we assumed that the claimed 325bhp was also the same. In fact it was 280bhp at 5500rpm, but the torque was correct; given that a good Vantage of the time peaked at 265bhp, it was a slightly warmed engine – the test report said, 'Standard engine well run in, special head with modified seats and ports, valve timing standard'. Ah well, we live and learn, but doubtless it would now be called blueprinting.

It had been the company's intention to follow up the 1967 launch of the DBS with the introduction of the V-8 the following Motor Show, but the effort for the small design and development team – only 22 people – in getting the new car into production, left inadequate time for a full DBS V-8 development programme, and it was deferred for another year. So the 1968 Motor Show saw nothing new from Aston Martin; the DB6 was offered at £4497 including tax, the Volante at £5062 and the DBS at £5718 – the latter £219 more than the previous year, entirely due to an increase in purchase tax. By contrast the AC 428 Fastback was £5426, the Bristol 410 £5997, a Ferrari Daytona £8563, Maserati Sebring 3500 £6553 and a Rolls-Royce Silver Shadow £7790. The basic Mini was by now £561.

Heart of a V-8

Thoughts on a replacement for the Marek 6-cylinder started not long after it went into production, before even the DB5 was launched. David Brown was after even more performance than the DB5 could offer, but performance of a more effortless kind, not only for the engine but for the car's occupants too. That would need a bigger car, so the new engine had to cater for increased weight and frontal area with a bit in hand to keep the company ahead in the high performance league. It was known that Jaguar was working on a V-12; Aston Martin hadn't enjoyed its Lagonda V-12 experience; Ferrari then used nothing but V-12s for road cars; V-8s were popular in America and non-existent in Europe apart from the big Maserati which only had a racing application at the time.

Thus Marek started on the design of the new V-8 in 1963. Ten per cent on frontal area meant ten per cent more power, while an increase in maximum speed from 150 to 160mph meant another 20 per cent increase, or 32 per cent total, given the same drag factor. That increase when applied to capacity, gave 5.28-litres for the equivalent normal DB5 tune at 317bhp and Vantage tune of 352bhp, by scaling up the 240 and 267bhp which were the true figures against the claimed 282 and 325 for triple SU/triple Weber DB6.

And so the V-8 was designed to range from 4.6 to 5.4-litres. Having become caught in the exaggerated horse-power race throughout the life of the DB4/5/6 in an effort to match freak American figures, Aston Martin never quoted figures for the V-8. However, as Dudley Gershon's book has published true development figures, and current German laws require true figures now, I will stick to development figures from the actual factory test sheets, which usually held their readings for at least ten seconds. In fact the figures are very comparable to those of today, but it must be remembered that these are harder to come by now when meeting current emission levels.

Marek's brief was to retain as much of the six-cylinder thinking and components as possible; that meant keeping piston, valving, cam shapes, valve gear and bearing sizes as start-points. Of course it had to retain twin overhead cam-shafts per bank, and had to be in aluminium, as American thin-wall cast-iron was still in its infancy. So drawing started in 1963 with 64° valve-angle – the 80° of the DB4 rejected for its greater width. Three chains were used on the intermediate sprocket plus one to each bank, a total of 12 sprockets in all, including top

Cutaway drawing of the V-8 at the time of its announcement in January 1967 in 5-litre form and undisclosed horsepower. Twin ohc per bank and four downdraught Webers are obvious features of the light alloy unit.

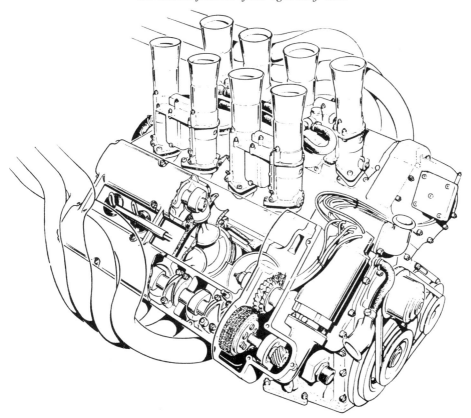

Early cranks had trouble with loose plugs; here Mick Wilson cleans out the hole prior to inserting the plug.

Current front end design has changed little since 1967; skew gear on left hand camshaft is for distributor drive. Fred Waters is checking valve timing.

tensioners and the underslung oil pump. To enable the carry-over principle to work, the bore was initially fixed at the same 96mm as the 4-litre while an 83mm crankshaft gave 4806cc; in the six cylinder the bore had ranged from the DB4's 92mm 3670cc, to the MP212 98mm at 4164cc, both with the 92mm stroke, so the new unit was setting out to overcome increased frictional losses with increased revability from the shorter stroke. There was little choice but to make the crankshaft to a two-plane design for the inherently better secondary balance; the single plane has good primary balance and 90° pulsing, but poor secondary balance, which places a premium on engine mounts or lower revs. In his drafting Marek was assisted by Alan Crouch on the details.

While the various ancillaries came in first and were given their own proving trials it wasn't until June 1965 that the block and heads arrived from the casting company; two years may seem a long interval between first putting pen to paper and receiving the ready-to-assemble article, but it must be remembered that Marek was one of 23 engineers who also had day-to-day duties to perform on general development of existing products, and foundry lead times are long when they have to build patterns as well. By then the engineering department no longer had their own machine shop – which they had had at Feltham – and had to scrounge time from production. However it was all assembled – albeit with a lower than intended 8.36:1 compression ratio.

On Thursday, July 29th, 1965 the first V-8 started at 2.30pm; it was a little rich on its 46IDA Webers, there was an electrical fault and the damper was rubbing on the front of the timing case. Running in continued the following day. After the week-end the engine was partially stripped; the bearings looked good, but the Renolds tensioner to the oil pump drive required modification.

It was back on the bed again on the Tuesday; the tensioner modification had worked and the engine was running perfectly. The following day saw the first power curve taken; it reached 275bhp at 5750rpm, but wouldn't pull below 2500rpm until the emulsion tubes had been changed. Come the following Monday, experiments were made on the bore size of the two-piece manifolds and jetting. By the end of the day the engine had clocked 40 hours of total running and recorded 285bhp at 6000rpm with a peak bmep of 141.5psi (275lb ft) at 4500rpm. In fact the torque curve stayed over 250lb ft from 3000-

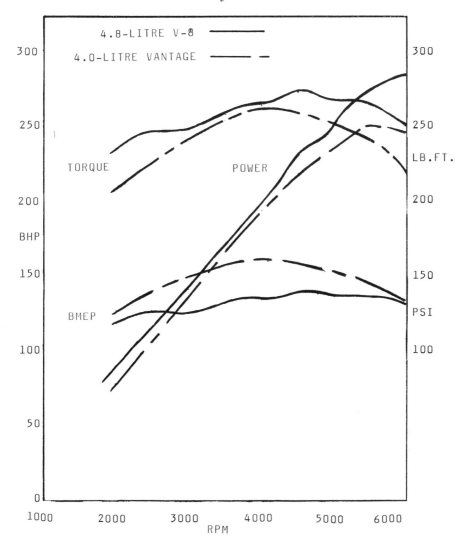

First power curve was taken on August 9th, 1965 and is here compared with an average 4-litre Vantage. While the BMEP shows the V-8 less efficient at this stage, the extra 0.8-litre gives it more overall torque and a useful power increase.

6000rpm. The bmep was close at 2000 and 6000rpm to that for an average Vantage, so the carry-over principle was working. Now these figures have come from engineer George Evans' personal record of the time, carefully tabulated and dated, and he was in the test house! Curiously, Marek's internal record gave the correct horsepower, but gave an artificial lift of 20psi to the bmep, whether by mistake or artifice cannot now be discovered. Dudley Gershon's '325bhp on the second day' wasn't to come for another four months! And the 385bhp from GT profile cams wasn't recorded until half way through the following year, and that was with a 5-litre.

That isn't to belittle the early performance of the V-8.It did straight away what it set out to do – match the efficiency of its forerunner and provide a sound basis for further development. It is a tribute to Marek's design skill that it was able to do this within four testing days of first starting, and it does not require any exaggeration.

After the tests on the bed it was stripped for inspection. Pistons were in good shape and bearings had only suffered from some pitting from dirty castings. The cam chains had been fouling the top cover so that was relieved, and the heads were fine, apart from exhaust valves that had tuliped by some 0.005in – these were exchanged for the 6-cylinder valve material KE965. In the rebuild 0.036in was taken off the head to bring the compression ratio to the designed 9:1.

The next tests showed 297bhp at 6000rpm from which Metalastik later confirmed the choice of the 6-cyl torsional vibration damper. During oil pressure tests after that, a con-rod bolt failed at 6000rpm which caused a certain amount of internal mayhem; in fact it happened just after the engine had been up to 6500rpm for the first time. It was shown that the bolts had not been properly heat-treated and lost their elasticity; their diameter had been the same as that of the six-cylinder, design had been similar and the loads were lower – it shouldn't have failed. The rest of the bolts were sent away for proper heat treatment and the engine reassembled with a certain amount of welding, while the oil gallery was bad enough to require sleeving. Crankshaft, two rods, two pistons and liners and three valves had to be replaced.

Back on the bed towards the end of September, the engine was very carefully run in for 40 hours on light load, and it then continued for carburetter testing, but at the end of the month it failed again. Of the two possible causes – another rod bolt or a piston breaking across the gudgeon pin – Hepworth's pin-pointed the rod bolt for a variety of accepted reasons. The threads were then found to be inaccurately cut, so aircraft specification Unbrako bolts were fitted.

Back on the bed again on the 25th October, the unit continued where it left off at 296bhp. Fabricating a 1-to-3, 2-to-4 exhaust manifold with the same cam timing as before, recorded the first move over 300bhp – 310bhp at 6000rpm with peak bmep still at 141psi at 4500rpm. November 1965 saw a steady series of tests on cam timing and carburetter settings, bringing the power up to 319bhp at 6000rpm. The following month saw this up to 325bhp at 6000rpm and bmep up to 165psi at 4500rpm (318lb ft). Removing an inch from the manifold length to ease car installation dropped 6bhp.

On December 27th – no long Christmas shut-downs then – fuel injection was tried for the first time; this was the AE Brico system, still very much in its infancy; it was to be another four years before it was offered on the DB6. Complete with small computer it operated on a sequential system of one squirt per bank which sounds far less efficient than practice proves; the 4.8-litre V-8 recorded 317bhp at 6000rpm and 160psi bmep – not far behind the 46mm down draft Webers, but more important was the 4-inch reduction in overall engine height. At the same time distributor advance curves were sent to Lucas to be matched for Opus ignition. By now the Unbrako bolts had run for 93 hours, so that problem was reckoned to be cured. During this time a second engine was being built up. However the first engine continued until it had clocked 100 hours before being stripped again. Conrods themselves were all in good condition, as were their bearings, but the final main showed signs of starvation and the B-bank liners showed signs of scuffing.

Starvation of the rear main was due to loosening crank plugs while the B-bank scuffing, a V-8 problem, was attacked by holes drilled into the big-end eye at about 30° to the vertical, pointing at B-bank. The revised rods were fitted to the second engine which ran at the end of January 1966 with the same overlap cams as the first unit; its 320bhp showed consistency. After a month of air-cleaner and carburetter testing, this had increased to 329bhp at 6200rpm with the 46IDA3 Webers carrying 40mm chokes rather than 38mm; bmep was up to 168psi, but at 4750rpm. Comparable figures on the AE system were 325bhp but the torque was a little stronger from 3-4000rpm. Meanwhile, one engine had been installed in MP222, the uprated DB5 registered NPP7D, with a power bulge on the bonnet to clear the downdraft carburetters, together with a rather poor steering lock; the

Early con-rods had trouble with the drilling of the oil way; here Dick Shepherd uses a jig to get the angle right.

necessary wishbone shortening didn't actually improve the handling, but that wasn't the point of the test.

It was hardly surprising that the thoughts of Aston engineers were once again turning towards competition; it was after all just over two years since the end of the 214/215 era, and Ford had embarked on successful use of a developed production engine with push-rods! The mists of time rather disguise who approached whom, but in March 1966 a 5.9-litre Chevrolet engine, as used in the Can-Am Lola T70s, was borrowed from John Surtees. Doubtless to a certain amount of surprise, the engine, weighing in at 540lb with starter and flywheel, less exhaust and dynamo, produced 412bhp from 6200-6500rpm and 398lb ft of torque (165psi bmep) at 4500rpm, but over 350lb ft from 4000-6100rpm. Its specific fuel consumptions ranged from 0.56 pints/ bhp/hr at 5000rpm to 0.670 at the peak 412bhp.

While the racing involvement should arguably be a separate story, it was such an important part of the V-8 development that it must be retained in this chapter in its chronological place.

At the time, of course, the Aston V-8 was still only 4.8-litres and had seen no higher than 325bhp, but the Chevrolet gave a vital yardstick in outright power; it was however, never an endurance engine. Thus with the figures in mind, but not circulated to the management until matched, work continued on two fronts, ultimate performance and driveability. Shortly afterwards one of the development engines was stretched to 5-litres using a 97.75mm bore with the same 83mm stroke to give 4983cc. Within a few days of the first run-ups of the 5-litre version, it was tried with cross-over 45DCOE Webers on the basis that such carburetters were each £7 cheaper than the 46IDA; they eliminated a 2000rpm flat-spot and they dropped the overall engine height by 2¼ inches.

Horsepower was now up to 332bhp at 5500rpm on 40mm chokes. The final curve before the engine was installed in DP200 – the de Dion DB4 registered 4YMC – showed 322bhp at 5500rpm on 38mm chokes with 171psi bmep at 4000rpm (335lb ft of torque). This car immediately embarked on the same series of high speed road miles to build up experience. Initial figures from the car were 13.8mpg and 2800mpg of oil. Marek wanted to send the car on a major Continental exercise to gain greater knowledge of installed temperatures and their

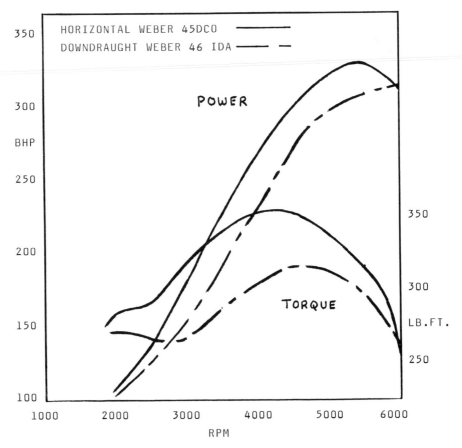

Marek's report of June 1st, 1966 compared performance of downdraught and cross-over horizontal Webers. Cross-overs not only gave more power at 330bhp against 315bhp but eliminated the worst of the mid-range flatspot; 45 DCOEs were cheaper too.

relationships, but a caustic comment in his report states that management refused to allow such expense!

Meanwhile the first engine for Surtees went on the bed on May 26th, 1966, rising from 322bhp through 375bhp with GT profile camshafts to a final figure of 421bhp at 6500rpm with more extreme camshafts and 44mm chokes in 48IDA Webers, with 386lb ft of torque at 5000rpm (192.5psi) – more power but slightly less torque than the bigger capacity Chevrolet – while the specific fuel consumptions ranged from 0.557 pints/bhp/hr at 5000rpm to 0.577 at 6500rpm, noticeably better than the American unit. The high-lift cams required the piston tops to be

Cross-over manifolding allowed the engine to be installed in an otherwise standard DBS without raising the bonnet bulge.

machined, bringing the compression ratio down to 9.1:1 and a Vertex magneto was used as the Lucas equipment had too much spark scatter over 6000rpm. Off the bed the engine was stripped and inspected. Bearings were all good but the crankshaft plugs still showed a tendency to unscrew. Further, the last two cylinders on A-bank were running hotter than the rest which was put down to a biassed water pump; however this was causing some detonation between 3000 and 4000rpm, so further investigation was to continue.

During August 1966 this was installed in an open Lola T70. After nine laps the driver reported that there was some oil surge, but that the engine seemed to have tightened. They listened to a small knock, changed plugs and sent him on his way; the engine blew up next lap. A big end had torn away from its rod, suggesting either rod or cap failure. The bearing cap had a stress-raising sharp radius where it was machined to allow the bolt to seat, and it was assumed that this was the cause. Marek suggested that high power testing be postponed for 4-6 weeks while new, stronger caps were produced. The oil surge was due

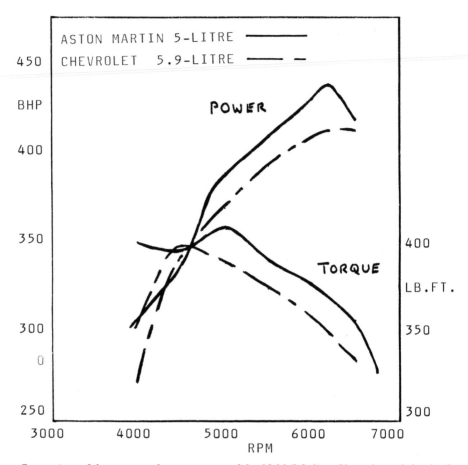

ASTON MARTIN 5-LITRE ————

CHEVROLET 5.9-LITRE ——— —

POWER

TORQUE

BHP

450

400

350

300

0

250

400

LB.FT.

350

300

3000   4000   5000   6000   7000

RPM

Comparison of the power and torque curves of the 1966 5.9-litre Chevrolet and the April 1967 Le Mans 5-litre. While the American unit delivered its power more cleanly, the Aston had more ultimate power and torque.

to the special flat sump fitted for the benefit of ground clearance – it was still a wet sump. Even inside Aston Martin it still seemed necessary to justify the fact that racing improves the breed, as Marek's report concludes: 'thanks to the development of the high power engine, it was possible to discover, and eliminate at an early development stage, a fault in design which could become very costly and unexplainable on normal production engines after they reached a long service life'. Fortunately the block and crankshaft were recoverable.

While this was happening a 4.8-litre engine with mild camshafts and 316bhp was being prepared to visit Weber in Bologna. Despite the downdraft carburation this was MP222. This was to cure the bottom end performance by revisions to the progression holes, emulsion tubes and butterfly angles, and it was successfully achieved so that the car performed well. At high speeds the water temperature stayed below 85° and the oil below 90°C. Unfortunately the customary fog around Bologna at that time of the year precluded maximum speed testing, but runs were made in Germany on the way back where the car recorded 158-160mph and was still accelerating. Consumption at 13.8mpg of oil was similar to that of the other car.

A dry sump lubrication system was designed and developed during October with two scavenge pumps and one pressure pump driven by chain on a single shaft below the crankshaft.

It was in this form that the Aston Martin V-8 was announced to the Press at the January 1967 Racing Car Show, and so too was the Lola T70 Mk. III GT. We announced the two in the same January 7th issue of *Motor*, but weren't allowed to couple them other than by quoting the rumours that abounded. We put the Aston announcement on the last half-page of the Lola announcement. Aston's information was pretty scanty; it gave bore and stroke at 98×83 which, for some reason that defies mathematical explanation, was always quoted at 5064cc; it actually comes to 5008.5cc with the benefit of a modern calculator. But Astons were still on the fractionally smaller bore at that time.

With its modified big-end caps, Surtees' engine was built up to the 421bhp specification with 48IDA Webers, GT exhaust cams and a special inlet profile of higher lift which had been used on the MP212/4/5 cars (0.051in higher), large inlet valves and dry sump lubrication. This was installed in an open Lola T70 for testing at Goodwood and Silverstone by David Hobbs and John Surtees. They liked the smooth feel of the engine but noticed a hesitation between 4000 and 4500rpm; despite poor weather the car wasn't that far off the lap record at either circuit. Then after 300 racing miles (on top of 40 hours bed testing previously), a connecting rod broke.

Analysis of the failure suggested that either the bolt had failed, leading to the opening of the big-end eye, followed by cracking across the lubricating hole in the shoulder, or vice versa. After exhaustive stress and fatigue fracture tests it was discovered to be the latter – rough drilling of the two holes from opposite ends had led to stress fracture.

As a result a pair of holes was moved to the less stressed area at the top of the big end either side of the H-section and the shoulder was thickened, adding some 2¼oz to the weight, a modification which went straight into the pre-production engines for which the balance was corrected. It also emerged that the forgings were far from perfectly symmetrical, so racing rods were built up from hand forgings and fully machined. Thus a second engine was supplied to Lola with revised heads to allow the same high-lift inlet cam to be used for the exhaust side, fully machine modified rods and a forged assembly of 98mm bore, plus the other changes on the earlier engine. In its optimised form with megaphones and open pipes, it gave 450bhp at 6000rpm with 413lb ft of torque and 205psi bmep at 5000rpm. While this was going on, there was still time to prepare an engine to send to Bosch for production mechanical injection development.

In an attempt to predict the potential performance at Le Mans, a Lola T70GT was taken to MIRA wind tunnel on February 21st and 22nd, 1967. In its basic unfinned state the car's drag factor came out at 0.453; various combinations of front and rear ride height, front and rear spoilers, front undertray and filling in the valley over the engine were tried. While the range of drag factor went from 0.423 to 0.503 the lift variation was even greater, the front always positive, ranging from a mere 9lbs to 390lbs at 200mph, the rear always negative from 421 to 687lb of downforce at the same speed. In fact the lowest drag version had 69lb of lift at the front and 481lb negative at the rear using a lowered front with fins and an extended upsweep at the tail. On the basis of this drag factor with an 85 per cent transmission efficiency, Marek reckoned the car would be good for almost 200mph.

Based on the then available information it was announced the following month, March, that there would be two Lola Astons at Le Mans, although at that point the revised engine had had little endurance testing.

Surtees had his next engine in mid-March and this was put into the T70GT for the first time. The first test was at Snetterton and Surtees wasn't too happy; he complained that the engine felt rough, with considerable vibration around 6000rpm, and that it wouldn't pull over 6100rpm in top gear. The test stopped short when a faulty valve spring cracked a tappet. New ones were on order but not yet ready, so special

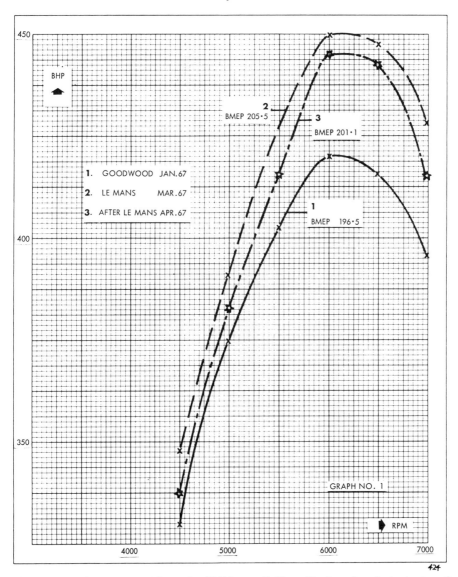

Comparison of power curves shows the 420bhp available at Goodwood at the beginning of 1967 rising to the 450bhp at the start of the Le Mans test week-end. Following the post-Le Mans rebuild the engine had dropped only 5bhp.

hand-wound ones had to be produced for the car to go to the Le Mans test week-end. Surtees took the one car to the French circuit and on the dry Saturday was third fastest behind a couple of Ferraris, but ahead of the Mk. II Fords.

On the Sunday he was fastest in the wet. So things were looking promising but the engine was still not feeling right and wouldn't pull higher than 6100rpm in fifth; dropping the gearing produced no change – 6100rpm was the limit. The wet Sunday, plus other spoiler changes and incidents, didn't allow any further investigation of the engine's oddities, and finally one of the suspect valve springs broke.

Back at the factory, and with its valve spring replaced, the engine was soon showing 445bhp, which after 800 racing miles and 40 hours of bench testing, showed that it wasn't really the engine's fault; it had to be something to do with the installation: either the drag factor was not as predicted, or the intakes were getting starved at high speeds. A return visit to MIRA was needed. While this deliberation was going on the third engine was built up with the 450bhp specification but with Lucas fuel injection which gave it 437bhp and 200psi bmep.

A further modification was the trial use of alloy bearing caps. The main bearing caps were designed in steel but had never shown any adverse results of differential expansion. At an early stage the block outer faces had been ribbed, to alleviate liner fretting but, generally, the block was thought to be pretty sound at the start of 1967. Then one of the production engines displayed cracks around its centre bearing housing to be followed by another, hence the precaution of trying Dural bearing caps in case the differential expansion had induced stress – the cap bolts were dowelled – but cracks subsequently appeared in other engines. The racing engines didn't seem to have suffered, but Dural caps were put in Surtees' engine, delivered on April 22nd just in case. After some more Snetterton testing, it returned to the factory bench on May 4th with three broken valve springs. It was rebuilt with Cooper rings and gaskets to 438bhp; someone must have been worried by a gasket failure which didn't earn a mention in the internal reports.

During the same week, and only a month before Le Mans, Aston Martin had taken a Lola GT back to MIRA to try and discover why the engine suffered apparent starvation at high speed and wouldn't give more than 186mph, whereas a Chevrolet powered car had reached the same speed at Spa where the Lola Aston should have made its debut on May 1st – lack of fuel injection was given as the reason for that not occurring.

The baseline was established with the car in Spa trim with a drag

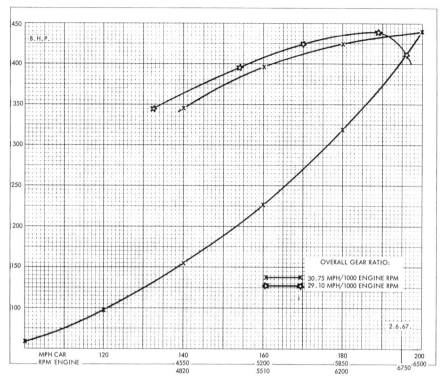

450
B.H.P.
400
350
300
250
200
150
100

OVERALL GEAR RATIO:

30.75 MPH/1000 ENGINE RPM
29.10 MPH/1000 ENGINE RPM

2.6.67.

MPH CAR   120   140   160   180   200
RPM ENGINE   4550   5200   5850   6750 6500
                                  4820   5510   6200

Endeavouring to predict the Lola-Aston's maximum speed at Le Mans showed that it should reach 200mph given the right drag factor.

factor at 0.472. Removing the rear bodywork altogether produced a remarkable 0.351, but reduced the rear negative lift to almost nothing. Using a modified rear body with shortened buttresses behind the cockpit and a covered 'valley' between them, plus a lowered deck behind the rear wheel arches, produced 0.376 but with too little rear downforce. However the simple answer of adding a full width 4 inch spoiler to that gave the required negative lift but also, somehow, found some front downforce that increased the drag factor to a wind-stopping 0.506. And it was in that guise the car ran at the test week-end, obviously considerably different from the 0.423 used for the calculations. Given 450bhp and the 0.506 drag factor, the 186mph maximum was all that could be expected – just the same as a 421bhp Chevrolet with a 0.472 drag factor at Spa, suggested the conclusion. Therefore would Mr. Broadley and Mr. Surtees please reduce the drag factor to

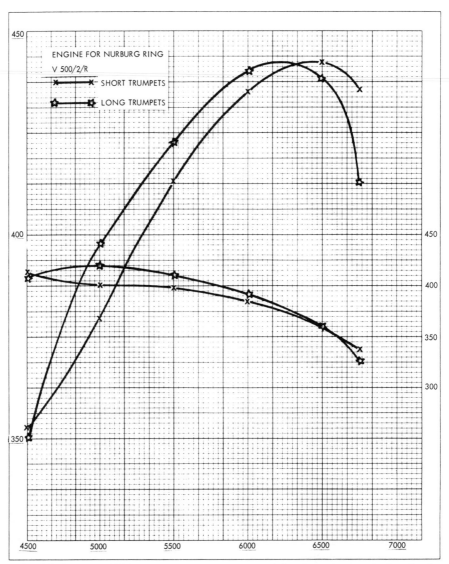

For Nurburgring 1967 two power curves were available depending on the length of trumpets fitted to the downdraught carburetters. Theory is confirmed by the better torque of the longer trumpets.

something like the 0.376, and the 450bhp Aston should give 206mph. And so time marched inexorably towards Le Mans. Meanwhile Surtees, with David Hobbs as co-driver, elected to go to the Nurburgring 1000Km a fortnight before the 24-hour race. Practice saw

122

the car second fastest behind the Chaparral; unfortunately that wasn't as impressive as it sounds as neither Ford nor Ferrari were present. In the race Surtees was slow away when the engine wouldn't fire immediately, but was up to seventh by the end of the second lap with the Chaparral and a squad of Porsche 910s ahead. Then after six laps the rear wishbone broke halfway down the notorious Foxhole and the car skated to a frightening halt, mercifully undamaged. It was regarded as a promising start.

A day or two later the No. 1 Le Mans engine was back on the bed and in installed trim produced the accepted 438bhp at 6500rpm; the ex-Nurburgring engine showed just under 400bhp on the test-house exhaust system, while a spare produced 410bhp in the same state.

Now, some twenty years later, it isn't easy to elicit in what frame of mind the team went to Le Mans; how seriously they were taking the possibility of cracked crankcases, how confident they were that they had had anything like enough full load endurance testing. In hindsight and not just from an analysis of the results – there just hadn't been enough continuous running, no evidence of even a 12-hour cycling run. They had had their teething problems, certainly, and cured them as they came. The Surtees/Broadley team too must have had their reservations over the lack of car testing, although Hawkins' fourth at Spa with a Lola-Chevrolet, plus all the experiences gained with the open Can-Am cars, justifiably gave them reasonable confidence that their end of the combination had something solid behind it. However, reading between the lines of internal reports the relationship between Astons and the Surtees/Broadley axis was becoming a little strained.

The two Lola-Astons were to be driven by Surtees/Hobbs and Irwin/de Klerk. On scrutiny the cars weighed in at 1060Kg – almost identical to that of the Nimrod-Astons 15 years later. Come first practice and it was obvious that the Lola team had done their aerodynamic homework, as both cars pulled 6300-6400rpm down the straight. Plugs were acceptable, but harder ones were substituted for safety; oil and water temperatures were in good order. The engines needed nothing more than a brief checkover.

Come second practice the following evening, and the No. 2 car immediately developed overheating – a failed gasket. However the Surtees car was going well – 6500rpm down the straight and then 6700 with a tow—Marek's projected 205mph.

But towards the end of practice this car too had to be brought in with head gasket failure. There is no doubt that the Mulsanne places a considerable strain on a car and in-car installations are never quite the same as the test-bed, but two gasket failures must have been a little worrying; that the concern must have arisen earlier is shown by the fact that there were new gaskets of the latest pattern to hand, complete with shims to put under the rings.

The engine rebuilds were left to the Aston mechanics who worked through the Thursday night. All heads were in good condition on which both Broadley and Surtees commented.

With the engines rebuilt by mid-day Friday the cars were tested on the road and agreed to be race-ready; they were both driven to the circuit the following day.

The team had a little drama in front of the pits just before the off when the second car displayed gear linkage trouble, but this was rectified in time. Surtees completed the first lap in eighth place and was

The Lola Aston in present day guise is seen at Silverstone during an historic race.

seventh at the end of the second lap, but at the end of the third lap he pulled into the pits with a loss of power. All plugs bar one were in good condition, but that one had aluminium all over it and it was obvious that a piston had melted.

The second car did 10 laps before the fuel pump cogged belt drive pulley failed due to fracture of the drive shaft from the camshaft. One was cannibalised from the team's spare engine and the car went on its way. A lap later it was back with the flange on the cam-pulley detached; this was repaired quickly and, for 20 laps at around 3 minutes 40 seconds, the car seemed to have recovered. But then it stopped with bad vibration and low oil pressure. And that was that, a disastrous Le Mans for Aston Martin, but nevertheless a valuable exercise.

For the failure of the faster car, Surtees blamed the injection for going weak, and the team blamed Surtees for his last minute change of plugs to those of a different manufacturer. In that the second car was actually running weaker, and that the other seven plugs in his own engine indicated a satisfactory mixture, Surtees was probably wrong, and it is almost certain that the Aston team were right, but there is equally no doubt that the engine was not fully proven to be race-worthy.

Back at the factory both engines were stripped. The second engine showed the dreaded cracks around main bearing housings and between the base of a pair of cylinders; whether this had allowed sufficient oil pressure loss for the bearings to wear and let the crank vibrate, in turn breaking the damper, isn't clear – nor if the cause was in fact the unbalanced forces of the heavier big-ends. The Surtees engine showed a neat hole in a piston crown which had transferred a lot of its metal onto the exhaust valve. All other pistons and liners looked shiny new and the heads displayed no sign of weak mixture.

As the Aston team had still not completed a decent endurance run with the high-power engine, and needed more such information, they built up the Surtees engine to Le Mans specification again with just two new pistons, a new exhaust valve and four Dykes oil control rings. Head gaskets were again fitted with shims (0.0085in) under the Cooper rings and the water holes were surrounded by soft solder wire.

It wasn't possible to do a continuous 24-hour run due to the noise in a built-up area, nor to do a full eight hours in a day, as smoke affected either the Service department or the Engineering department – then

The inside of Surtees's Le Mans engine following the holed piston after just three laps; melted aluminium has coated the combustion chamber and the exhaust port, ruining the valve seat in the process.

occupying the whole of the round-roofed building known as Olympia. They did five hours a day as a compromise which also allowed the water brake time to cool down.

The test started on July 13th with 2½ hours of light load up to 3000rpm, followed over the next two days by a further five hours before running in was considered complete. The endurance run was at constant ¾-load with 15 minutes at 5000, 5500, 6000, 5000rpm etc with occasional bursts to 6500rpm. The first test lasted 27½ hours, at

126

Following the break-up of the block casting around the main bearings, the caps were deepened and the block buttressed to sandwich them. Frank Matthews torques down a cap nut.

127

which point water started to appear from the first and second cylinders on B bank.

Inspection showed that the block had cracked between these two cylinders and a crack had also appeared across the main bearing stud on the opposite side. It was decided that this was a function of the main bearing studs whose dowel sections were transmitting lateral forces into the main bearing diaphragm rather than out to the walls of the block – an extension of the pre-Le Mans fears. Arguably the lateral forces were a function of the secondary out-of-balance of the larger big ends, which may have had a greater effect than was realised at the time. Accordingly the block was rapidly redesigned to give lateral location to new bearing caps – once more also in Dural as the common expansion rate had become essential.

The engine was back together again to start on August 15th for another 25-hour run. Stripping revealed no cracks. It was then reassembled for another 25-hour run with a new water pump and one new oil ring; the test was stopped after 24¾ hours when water appeared in the exhaust system following a power loss. Stripping again revealed no cracks and all bearings were in excellent condition, as was everything else, including the new Borg Warner automatic chain tensioner.

The power loss had been due to a loss of valve clearances in B-bank which had led to a hair crack between the ports on the back cylinder, hence water loss. The valve clearance closing was thought not to be serious after that length of endurance testing which covered more than one 24-hour race, but it is interesting to record that similar closure was happening when Aston returned to the racing scene 15 years later – now finally cured.

Marek concluded that the engine was strong enough to withstand any road or racing loads and was therefore releasable for production, once a production piston had been developed with less slap and lower oil consumption; this was started the following month. He further suggested that the oil pump had an unnecessarily high throughput and could do with a size reduction to save power and reduce oil temperatures.

While the Le Mans performance was outwardly a rather extravagant and public failure, it nevertheless proved once more that racing improved the Aston breed far faster than any road testing ever would.

Whatever individual members of the team may have felt about their version of the reasons behind the failure of Surtees' engine, the failure of the second engine was a fundamental design fault, and it must be acknowledged that, if it hadn't been for Broadley and Surtees, the engine would not have had its rapid development through racing.

Meanwhile work on the production version quietly continued on the carburation front. Following the testing of the AE Brico set-up, which had first been undertaken back in December 1965, further testing had taken place in April 1967, and the engine had been installed in old faithful 4 YMC for AE to programme the driveability settings. This had now returned to Newport Pagnell with 323bhp and 275lb ft of torque from 2000-5750rpm, peaking at 320lb ft at 4200rpm. Compared with the DB6 the Brico-equipped V-8 proved more economical throughout the speed range in fourth gear than the DB6 in fifth. Comparing fifth gear figures the V-8 achieved 27mpg at 40mph (20 for DB6), 22mpg at 70mph (18½ for DB6) and 18½mpg at 100mph (14 for DB6). It was so flexible too that the car could pull away from idle in fifth gear and everyone who drove the car was very impressed. Marek stated that the sole question was over the injection reliability and that it should be left in the car to build up as many miles experience as possible.

At the same time Aston was also working with Bosch. In October 1967 the Bosch equipped engine had been some 15bhp down on the 46IDA version, but this was felt to be due to overly small butterflies and ram pipes. Bosch went away to perfect this while Aston was to develop a manifold capable of passing enough air for 350bhp.

Over the same period, under MP229, AML had been developing the DB6 to pass the Federal emission and, with the Stromberg Duplex system, were about to embark on the 50,000-mile durability test in December 1967; on the basis that this was expected to pass and the V-8 produced better fuel consumption already with the AE system, Marek concluded that the V-8 should have few problems.

Through to April 1968 much of the test-bed time was spent in optimising the Brico system using different length ram pipes and butterfly systems, until, by mid-April, the unit could reach 310bhp at 6000rpm and 340lb ft torque (168psi) at 4000rpm with hotter exhaust camshafts, but most of the time it was running below 300bhp, lower than the unit in 4YMC. By now of course, the DBS was in production and able to provide a real working test-bed. It had been established that the actual drag coefficient was a rather high 0.422 against the DB6 0.364, the frontal area was 22.1sq ft against 20.96sq ft while the six-cylinder version was some 200lb heavier than the 29.3cwt DB6. Thus, just to match the DB6 maximum speed would need 310bhp; to reach 160mph – the target for the four-seater, as opposed to the 170mph two-seater, needed 350bhp. The lower figure was easily attainable on the AE system but the higher figure, envisaged for a Vantage version, still needed carburetters or perhaps the Bosch system, which had still to be perfected back in April 1968. Spot checks on emission showed the 310bhp unit to be near the legal limits on CO and HC, which would have precluded the Vantage version from being allowed into the USA with the necessary greater overlap. Meanwhile an Italian run, in a Brico-equipped DBS V-8, confirmed drag figures with a 154mph maximum speed, but returned a disappointing 8.2mpg and 80 miles per pint of oil with high oil temperatures.

The Bosch unit returned to the bed in September 1968 to give 308bhp against the carburetters at 313bhp and the Brico at just under 300bhp. With American legislation in mind the decision was finally taken to go for the Bosch system which was showing far greater consistency of results; it was a blow to Brico, hardly alleviated by the option of its use on the DB6 Mk. II. At that time Weber couldn't match the emission levels and injection of one sort or another seemed to be the only answer for the US.

At that point the best installed figures for any tractable roadworthy set-up so far tried were around 315bhp; it was decided, at the close of 1968, to increase the capacity to 5340cc by increasing the bore to 100mm and the stroke to 85mm. Thus work continued on piston development during 1969.

In March the first of the 5340cc engines – V535/001/PX went to Bosch complete with cast inlet manifolds, air filters and airbox with a 9:1 compression ratio with 343bhp at 5500rpm. The second unit with downdraught Webers and standard camshafts was producing 365bhp at 6000rpm, while GT profile inlet cams gave 395bhp at 6000rpm, both tests with a 9.5:1 compression. A third engine in its most driveable form with carburetters gave 384bhp at 5800rpm before being installed in a DBS for a further Italian run. By the time the engine finally went into production following the October 1969 launch, the V/540 series was standardised at 310-320bhp developed at 5000rpm with only a slight fall-off at 5500rpm and 358lb ft at 4000rpm.

Tadek Marek (right) retired before his V-8 went into production but he visited the factory shortly afterwards to approve it and again when Mike Loasby (left) was in charge of the engineering.

It had been a long haul from the start of design in 1963, through the first runs in 1965 and the compressed development of the Le Mans 1967 exercise, but it was worth it. In substantially similar form it is still the same engine that is in use today.

Tadex Marek had retired during 1968 and thus never saw his engine into production, although he approved of the result when he tried a DBSV-8 a couple of years later. He left behind a superb engine painstakingly developed with a bottom end capable of sustaining a racing 575bhp in normally aspirated form and over 700bhp in twin-turbo form. Even now it is still a tribute to his great design ability.

Chapter Eight

Space and Speed

With the DBS in steady production by the middle of 1968 and its body shape developed to a reasonable compromise of lift and drag, work next started on the possible effects of the greater power output. Thus a 5-litre V-8 was installed in one of the DBS prototypes for an extended road test exercise to Italy, which was reckoned to be the best venue for sustained high speed work.

The maximum speed attained was 154mph which is commensurate with the 310bhp 5-litre and the 0.422 drag factor. Further experiments were to be made on lift with pressure measurements on the undershield. Mike Loasby again did the report and had the Belgian run as his comparison. While the lift was judged acceptable on the 140mph DBS it rapidly became apparent that more work was needed to make the V-8 version stable at high speeds. This was eventually cured after further ¼-scale wind-tunnel work with the bluff chin and undertray that went into the 1969 production cars with a final drag coefficient of 0.384.

Further problems were noted with front damping which required stiffening to reduce patter. Tyre tests used four sets of Avons – two cross-ply and two radial – and one set of Pirelli radials. The Avon cross-plies weren't up to the speeds and started chunking, but the Avon 205×15 came out well; however Pirelli's GR70 VR15 became the recommended fitting. Avon's speed/temperature graph confirmed the lift that Loasby had measured on pressure sensors.

With very hard driving it also became apparent that the wire wheels weren't strong enough for the increased torque and lateral grip as the spokes loosened; subsequently Aston had its own alloy wheels designed. Brakes too needed further development to reduce their temperatures, hence ventilated versions, while the oil temperature was also too high, necessitating a reroute of the oil cooler system to full-flow. However the water temperature was staying nice and cool, albeit to the detriment of the heater whose modulator valves were also playing up.

There was enough here, coupled with the wind-tunnel work, to provide steady work up to the 1969 launch. Tunnel tests had confirmed the front end undershield shape and proved that there was greater extraction from a grille at the top of the boot lid than through the rear quarter vents. It also showed that the area around the vents in front of the doors was of negative pressure, although this wasn't sufficient to deter them from later drawing air in at that point to the heating system. While this was continuing, there had been time to construct a stretched V-8, a four-door with an extra foot in the wheelbase; this was to become MP230 – once more a Lagonda, albeit Aston Martin Lagonda. First

Before the DBS V-8 was launched, Sir David Brown had a 4-door version built with an extra foot in the wheelbase; here it is still on its original DBS wire wheels, although it was updated before being shown to the press in January 1970.

The DBSV-8 was launched at the 1969 Motor Show where Danish model Beeira Sector tries not to dent the aluminium panels. Bluff spoiler and alloy wheels can also be seen.

torsional tests showed this to be somewhat floppy so the side members were strengthened by additional boxing top and bottom and an extra box inboard. In all, this increased the torsional stiffness by nearly 70 per cent. While this car was completed and used by Sir David Brown (knighted in 1968), as well as being launched to the press in January 1970, it never went into production during Sir David's ownership.

So the DBS V-8 was finally launched in September 1969 alongside the DBS and the DB6 Mk. II; this had been introduced in July that year with wider DBS wheels plus flared arches, power steering as standard and AE injection as an option. Prices, including purchase tax, were £4798 for the DB6 Mk. II, £6112 for the DBS and £6897 for the DBS V-8. Once again the Aston was well received by the press, although road test cars were not to be available until 1971.

V-8 production got under way early in 1970 with engines 006-009

V-8 finally installed into the DBS with the Bosch fuel injection and a rather contorted manifold dropping down below the air-boxes and approaching them from underneath. Note early cam covers.

producing 310-320bhp, all at 5000rpm. With such variety of machinery going through the factory, the production side was considerably stretched and there were inevitable minor teething troubles, but some 250 V-8s were produced in the first year-and-a-half.

Motor's road test car had engine number 45 in chassis 41. Factory records show that that engine gave 338bhp at 5500rpm with slightly oversize inlet valves while the torque figure was 355lb ft at 4000rpm. At 2000rpm it was 315lb ft and at 6000rpm 294lb ft. While these were better than the early production engines through further air-cleaner development and longer ram pipes, Aston Martin appears to have told *Motor* that the peak torque was as much as 400lb ft with over 300lb ft from 2000-6000rpm; while the latter figures aren't too far out, the 400lb ft was somewhat overflattering!

Nevertheless the car did perform extremely well, able to reach 60mph in 5.9 seconds and 100mph in 13.8 seconds, figures comparable to those of the unashamed two-seater AC Cobra 289 and the TVR Tuscan. Maximum speed, finally achieved in England on an unopened section of the M4 thanks to the co-operation of the Ministry of Transport, was a mean 160.1mph at 6200rpm on the 3.54 final drive with the new ZF 5-speed gearbox. There were reservations though on the low speed torque; not only was there a certain amount of surge and snatch at low speed in high gears, but there simply wasn't the expected V-8 pull. In third gear the fastest 20mph increment was from 40-60mph in 3.9 seconds, equalled by that from 50-70mph with the 60-80 and 70-90mph figures only 0.1 second slower. As 40mph in third corresponded to 2250rpm it was felt to be rather a top-endy engine. Arguably some of that could have been due to larger inlets than standard, but equally Bosch had a bad batch of injection pumps which also affected the cold-starting, about which *Motor* also complained.

Comparison of the six cylinder and V-8 installed in consecutive Motor road test cars. The V-8 reached 160mph at 6150rpm while the six recorded 141.5 at 5450rpm. Despite the V-8 being over its power peak, the improvement over the DBS was greater than theory should justify.

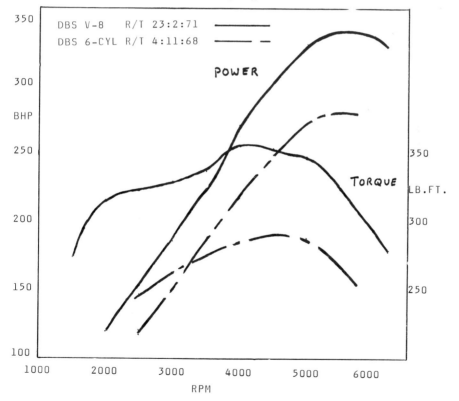

Apart from criticism of the heating, then in its multi-control phase, the rest of the test was full of superlatives – roadholding and brakes particularly; the power assisted rack was now provided by Adwest. The ride was reckoned good too, although bumpy corners could induce a diagonal pitch which was put down to poor Armstrong Selectarides on this car – they were to be replaced by conventional dampers shortly afterwards. Wet grip too earned a mild rebuke as the high speed 70 per cent Pirellis were reckoned to be inferior to the Avon radials on the DBS; however this was a function of the difficulty of finding any tyre to cope with 160mph performance for a car that in unladen form still weighed in at 34.5cwt.

There had to be some compromise – a problem that still rears its head. Yes, there were detail criticisms, but the overall impression was of a car that continued the best of Aston traditions – the fastest production four-seater with civilisation to match. By then the price was £7501. There was of course also an automatic transmission version for which the Chrysler Torque-flite was chosen.

Example of a production DBSV-8 with spoiler and bigger alloy wheels denoting its differences from the DBS.

With the car firmly accepted in Europe attention turned to getting the V-8 into America where emission control laws were fast gaining a foothold. These originally stemmed from the Los Angeles smog problem and it was California which led the rest of the country into the establishment of new laws. Those of the late sixties only governed carbon monoxide (CO) and hydrocarbon (HC) emissions which affected American cars from 1966 and imported ones from 1968. The actual figures were 275 parts per million of HC and 1.5 per cent CO after a 50,000-mile durability run; at that time a standard six-cylinder on triple SUs produced 728ppm HC and 3.9 per cent CO. Work started in 1967 on the DB6 engine to take three Stromberg CD emission carburetters with the Duplex inlet manifold, and to undercut the emission values by some 20 per cent to allow for deterioration during the 50,000 miles. Initial runs with these carburetters showed a loss of some 13bhp but gradual adjustments brought this up to scratch; finally with considerably reduced overlap on fresh camshafts, the figures were reduced to an acceptable level, albeit with some power loss in the end, back to 212bhp. The DB6 was laden to simulate the DBS and started its 50,000-mile test in December 1967. By May this had been completed with checks and servicing on the way and the emission levels were satisfactory, so a DBS went over to America and was duly certified; however this meant that the DB6 itself wasn't accepted in the US after that year.

Then the 1969 launch of the V-8 inevitably reached American ears which adversely affected sales of the DBS immediately. It mattered little that the V-8 wasn't ready for America for the laws of that year, let alone the tougher ones to come.

The V-8 finally managed to get into America by October 1971, still using the fuel injection, but with low compression and air injection following assistance from Ricardo, but it was to be short-lived as the engine then failed to match the requirements for the 1972 model year. By the time the new owners had taken control, 1973 had seen a demand for a reduction in nitrous oxides, a requirement that conflicts with that for reduced CO and HC levels.

In the meantime work was continuing on improving the DBS aerodynamics and, in March 1971, wind-tunnel tests were made on a modified body shape (MP231) which used a single headlamp per side, a

Wind tunnel model of MP231 showing the single headlights to be adopted later; the most significant feature is the higher tail designed to keep the air-flow attached for longer and reduce overall drag and rear lift.

roofline that fell away more quickly from the screen top towards a tail that retained the height of the kick-up over the rear wheel arch to give a less steep rear screen slope. The object of this was to keep the air-flow attached for longer, reducing the size of the wake and the rear lift. Other changes were a slatted air outlet vent on the rear quarter and transverse slats over the rear window. In its best form this reduced the drag from 0.384 to 0.358 without the front undertray; 160mph lift had been reduced from 396lb to 102lb at the front, and from 342lb to 183lb at the rear. While the undertray reduced the lift still further at the front, it increased it at the rear and the drag factor was higher. Blanking the radiator made no difference in that configuration. While this project 231 came to nothing as such, it was arguably the basis for William Towns's unadopted gullwing model, a two-seater coupé, and led to the following year's adoption of the single headlamp.

On the engine side, after much work on air cleaners and throttle positions, the department put the 288th engine on long term endurance

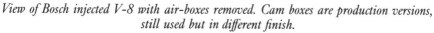

View of Bosch injected V-8 with air-boxes removed. Cam boxes are production versions, still used but in different finish.

testing in August 1971. No longer the so carefully assembled first production units, this was a typical sample after a year and a half of casting moulds and standard mass-production Bosch units. As received from production it gave 270bhp at 5000rpm after 5½ hours running in, but after only a little work on cleaning up the shape edges in the ports, it was markedly better, giving 294bhp at 5500rpm. Work was directed towards a number of areas – cam follower noise, exhaust valve failure and cylinder head gaskets. Experiments were made with 3-bearing camshafts, revised head studs, increased water passage areas and revised gaskets. Early September saw the unit at nearly 300bhp – they always improve with running. Then after considerable running a misfire developed on September 7th; an exhaust valve had burnt out and the spark plug electrode was eaten away. An inlet valve had also closed up its clearance.

Further tests were made on plugs and oil consumption with the engine now in cross-over inlet manifold form again with 45DCOEs; with minor jet and emulsion tube variations power was consistently around the 320bhp mark. Cam timing changes were tried to reduce petrol vapour blow-back. Then the Bosch system was put back and delivered 306bhp but the specific fuel consumptions were better than with carburetters below 4500rpm. By now a certain amount of disillusion had set in over the lack of adjustability of the Bosch system; if they wanted to try different camshafts it was back to carburetters to get the best comparative results, and this was certainly proving a problem over the preparation for emission tests, the very reason for which fuel injection had been chosen. Then, as now, it needs the injection supplier to be involved in any fundamental timing changes.

Further testing continued with the Bosch equipped engine; exhaust valve clearance was still a problem and various ways were tried of ensuring that the seats were properly shaped once the head was torqued down, while waterways were increased to improve exhaust port cooling.

Such problems in production engines inevitably beset a small company; however much time is spent in proving development engines, they still need more testing in production form. But by that time, shareholders are beginning to want to see a return on their investment and production has to go ahead; small wonder that there are occasional teething problems, especially in high performance engines.

The clearance problem was sorted out with revised seats and cooling passages while camshaft noise was to be taken out by the use of polynomial cams; ramps on the profile allow bigger basic clearances which will tolerate a certain amount of initial valve pocketing during the early life of the engine.

By late 1971 Weber had done its own research work on emissions and had come up with the 42CNF downdraught carburetter. These were straight away a power match for the older IDAs and DCOEs, and were soon better than the Bosch injection on specific consumptions (pints/bhp/hour). Lowering the compression ratio to 8.3:1 knocked some 20bhp off the power throughout a large part of the rev range, but this was a relatively small percentage; thus the way was pointed for further emission development, had the company not suffered its ownership hiccough.

The Motor Show that year saw the V-8 increased in price to £7640

Experimental car fitted with carburetters under the injection bonnet.

Many people visit the Newport Pagnell factory; some, like Twiggy, make more impression than others; Fred Hartley responds.

and the adoption of the Coolair air-conditioning system as standard, together with inertia reel seat belts, an 8-track stereo and a steering column lock.

News from the following month announced a future collusion between Aston Martin and BRM; they were to produce a new mid-engined sports car powered by the 3-litre BRM capable of taking on Ferrari and Lamborghini, and it was stated that 3000 would be produced per year. No prototype was ever built, although *Motor* suggested the body could well resemble the Siva project that Neville Trickett had shown at Earls Court that year using a midships Aston engine. Gull-winged and angular, it would have found little favour

144

among a clientele accustomed to the works of such as Frank Feeley, Touring, Zagato or William Towns.

Sadly all had not been well with the David Brown corporation. An expansion in tractor production had been followed by a drop in world-wide demand and the company could no longer afford to support Aston Martin as well. Obviously the lack of this had become apparent within the workforce, and a single entry among the blank pages at the end of one of George Evans' test books – not in his handwriting! – stated; 'If you make it this far in the book you will be very lucky before the firm pack(sic) up 17:11:71'.

As 1971 came to a close Sir David Brown sold Aston Martin Lagonda for an undisclosed sum to Company Developments, a Midlands investment company. It took until the beginning of March for the story to reach Press release state. William Willson became Chairman, G. E. Fletcher Managing Director, H. Pollack Technical Director and Charles Warden Financial Director. All were from the new company owners. Willson was definite that Aston Martin could be

The first Sotheby Special built by Ogle on a DBSV-8; this was bought by Embassy as a promotional vehicle. Most people preferred the original, however a replica was built on an AMV-8 chassis in January 1973.

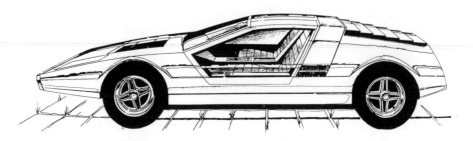

Neville Trickett designed and built this mid-engined Aston-powered Siva 530 for the Daily Telegraph; it was shown at Earls Court in 1971. This sketch is more flattering of the idea than the final car.

made into a sound company making cars at a profit, and that this could be achieved by financial expertise rather than by cheapening the cars. There was apparently no prospect of a return to sports car racing.

Thus ended the David Brown era, 25 years of achievement which established the marque in the top flight of luxury high performance cars. They had taken on the world in sports car racing and won in 1959; they had launched three new basic models over the years – DB2, DB4 and DBS with brand new engines for each – as well as three different Lagonda versions. Sir David left behind a legacy which has stood the marque well ever since.

Chapter Nine

New Blood

With the departure of Sir David Brown Aston Martin had lost a philanthropist; the new regime was determined to make the company self-supporting. Some of the old heads had gone too, most notably Dudley Gershon, but to the outside world the company carried on much as before and the engineering department was headed by Harold Beach. Their first move in April 1972 was to remove the DB nomenclature and to revise the front styling in line with the work on MP231 with single headlights; with the spare wheel laid flat they added more length to the boot, which was better for loading suitcases, even if the overall volume wasn't much different. Opus ignition became a standard fitting following earlier development. David Brown had produced some 405 DBS V-8s and 830 DBSs. Willson changed the chassis numbers to start at the next round number up on both models now labelled Aston Martin AMV-8 and AM Vantage. The prices, including tax, were £6950 for the six-cylinder and £8950 for the V-8 versions.

After a further 250 V-8s and only 70 six-cylinders a new version of the V-8 was launched in August 1973 and the 'six' was finally dropped. The new one, priced at £9593 which could easily be pushed over £10,000 with a sunshine roof and non-standard paint, was further refined with better engine and transmission cooling, interior revisions to seats, door locking, air extraction via a lip over the boot lid rather than the grille below the rear window, new sound deadening and other minor details. But the major change was the dropping of the Bosch injection in favour of the Weber 42DCNFs; externally the change was evident in the larger bonnet bulge which started with a larger intake and ran back to the rear of the bonnet.

147

Only a few months after taking over, Company Developments introduced the single headlight front end with the mesh grille; they named the surviving DBS six-cylinder models AM Vantage, with no lesser powered sister car.

The DBSV-8 was also renamed AM V-8 and restyled with the MP231 frontal treatment while the spare wheel was mounted horizontally to give more boot space.

Motor was quick to test a manual version of the new car and I managed to borrow that one for the third edition of *Classic Car* magazine. *Motor's* figures showed that the maximum speed was now 155mph at 5750rpm against the DBS V-8 at 160mph on the same final drive ratio; Avon's GR70 VR15 was now used instead of the Pirellis, and was fractionally larger in diameter.

Assuming the same drag factor, with some allowance for the fact that the slightly tuned DBS engine was further over its power peak, suggests that the AM V-8 engine was producing around 310bhp. Throughout the acceleration tests the two cars were almost identical with little more than 0.2 seconds between any standing start or high gear 20mph steps; however the newer car on the Webers was always slightly faster until the very top end with just that much more mid-range torque. Overall fuel consumption over the two very similar test exercises for the DBS V-8 and AM V-8, both with Continental runs, showed 12.9mpg for the

Revised switchgear and column mounted wiper stalk were features of the revised V-8 model introduced in August 1973. Apart from the air-conditioning controls the layout is much as we know it today.

Final production use of the six-cylinder engine was in this DBS, still complete with wire wheels and earless hub-caps.

Major change for the 1973 V-8 was the introduction of carburetters, once more downdraught Webers chosen for their ease of adjustment to meet American emission rules.

injection car and 14.7mpg on Webers. What was most noticeable, though, with the carburetted car was its light throttle behaviour; idling surge had gone and there was no snatch at steady low speeds in high gears – 30mph in fifth being 1200rpm. It made a disproportionate difference to one's enjoyment of the car as a whole.

In most respects it was a carefully refined version of the DBS V-8 with detail changes that were really effective. It was quieter, the handling was tauter without affecting the comfort of the high speed ride on undulating roads, the driver's locking switch for the passenger door was useful, even it it didn't ease the situation when opening the passenger's door first – perhaps a gentleman would have put a driver's door switch on the passenger's door instead!

Motor was not too happy with the weight of the clutch and the gearbox rattle at idle from the ZF box, but they didn't worry me unduly. Air conditioning, as mentioned in the previous chapter on the DBS, was

Carburetters required more under-bonnet clearance, so the power bulge was increased in size; the bumpers earned overriders.

by now the Coolair system which at that stage lacked controllability, and was inclined to provoke rather than prevent misting, and aimed its heat at the knees. But in every driving sense it was a pure Aston; magnificent performance, superb roadholding and a powerful masculine feel to the controls – an effortless grand tourer.

Priced at £9593 it had to compete against the 7.2-litre Jensen SP at £7320, the V-8 Maserati Indy at £9587, the Lamborghini Espada at £12,453, while the BMW 3.0CSL was just £7399 and the V-12 E-type a mere £3580, but the V-8 left them all behind on maximum speed and acceleration.

1973 was a bad year for industry. The after effects of the Yom Kippur war were the high oil prices and a rapid waning of interest in big thirsty cars. This was followed by the winter of discontent and the three-day week. Things were again looking bleak at Newport Pagnell. With a single-model policy they had geared up to produce some 10 cars a week – production had been totally integrated into the one factory before the end of the DB period; the declining demand and the lack of production on a full workforce put severe strains on the finances. The

One model policy with V-8s lined up in the panel shop prior to painting; by now the whole build operation took place at Newport Pagnell.

Before its move to the old R & D building, the trim shop was in the main factory.

Heath government fell in February and Harold Wilson returned, with Benn soon handing out cash to any troubled company that seemed ripe for conversion to the true socialist ideals of co-operative labour. Aston Martin applied for help.

Oblivious of the conflict between his own circumstances and those of his followers, the former Lord Standsgate was unable to assist an enterprise which so blatantly pandered to capitalist tastes. Help was refused.

In hindsight, this was a blessing; even at the time there must have been many an Aston owner who hoped the company wouldn't become part of the state-backed system. But the work-force, held at the ten a week level during these negotiations, had to be cut back in the face of declining home demand and the lack of American certification.

In the wake of the first reaction to the oil shortages, the company had thought seriously about closing down the American operation during 1973; it was felt that it was impossible for the big V-8 to meet the latest laws which introduced nitrous oxides emission levels that year.

However the American end was at that time run by Rex Woodgate who had worked with John Wyer in the racing days and had been asked to set up the importership at King of Prussia near Philadelphia in 1964.

Having survived the traumas of getting the DBS six-cylinder into the USA, only to have sales hopes dashed by the expectations of the V-8 which itself was only sellable for three months at the end of 1971, Rex promised to produce a set-up capable of passing the 1974 requirements. With the chance that this might happen came the realisation that the American market held one key to the replacement of the home market, so permission was granted. Four weeks and $4000 later, Rex and Ak Miller, a west-coast turbocharging specialist, had produced a turbo system with a 4-barrel Rochester and achieved the required results. This was seriously considered as a production possibility by the factory, but even more seriously by Weber Carburetters who rose to the

Faced with the prospect of no Astons for North America, Rex Woodgate produced an instant turbocharged version capable of passing the Federal laws; a single turbocharger was mounted in the vee to carry a 4-barrel Rochester carburetter (removed in this shot).

challenge. By this time the three-day week had come into being and progress was slow, so the decision was taken to attack the 1975 emission levels, which demanded lead-free fuel.

Early in 1974 Astons began to prepare for the American versions with special red-spot Webers, a later version of those that were being first run in the DB period back in 1971. Early runs in February were all at the sub-250bhp level but this eventually reached 268bhp. With the 1975 regulations further reducing the CO and HC levels, air pumps were used to inject air into the exhaust system, reducing the CO emissions by converting much of it to harmless CO_2. However it was still necessary to introduce catalytic converters into the exhaust system to oxidise CO and HC still further by lighting up the platinium coated ceramic honeycomb from exhaust gas heat. This development then went on to lead free fuel on an 8.3:1 compression ratio. With steady work this finally produced 275bhp at 5000rpm.

Quoting now my own paragraph in *Classic Car* after an October visit to Harold Beach at Newport Pagnell: *'While visiting Aston Martin to tie down the story of the Project cars (MP 212/4/5) I had the chance to see the engine that had come out of the V-8 that had been used to cover the 50,000 mile test for the American pollution laws. This has been rather critical for the Newport Pagnell firm as they have had a number of cars poised for export against passing this test. In fact it sailed through with flying colours including conforming to the more stringent Californian regulations; the route used for such an exercise includes some motorway travel but mostly on lesser roads with a spell on London's North Circular, all on lead-free fuel. The innards of the engine looked extremely clean, even the backs of the valve heads, bearings looked perfect and you could still see the honing marks in the bores. The sighs of relief from Newport Pagnell when it was all over must have sounded as if the research team were investigating steam power.'*

The V-8 duly received its certification in the 49 states and California, the latter certified on the 29th October, 1974, stating that 5-speed manual and 3-speed automatic transmission cars equipped with air pumps and oxidation catalysts were approved. America though was not the only market. The company had also established sales in Japan and Australia.

Earlier in the month of October, the Motor Show at Earls Court saw a new car unveiled. Sir David Brown's Lagonda finally saw the light of

155

At the end of September the V-8 finally completed its Federal certification 50,000-mile run and duly used the fact for advertising.

day. A luxurious five-seater using all the mechanical components of the AM V-8, it had the elegance that justified William Towns's principle of designing long for Lagonda and short for Aston. Priced at £14,040 in the UK against the Aston's £11,349, the Lagonda was to prove the swansong of Company Developments' period of ownership. Only four were built by the end of the year.

Company Developments were involved in the world of property and secondary banking; 1974 spelt a near disaster for many on both those counts. Although some money had been generated by the sale of the sports field and social club on the south side of Tickford Street for building development, and the company's collection of old cars had been sold along with much of the pre-DB4 parts and patterns, Willson's company could no longer afford the money or management time to keep Aston Martin going. That he was unsuccessful in his determination to prove that Astons could make cars and a profit, was not Astons' fault – the cards of the time were stacked against them.

At the end of 1974 the employees were summoned and told that the end had come – again. Rather than place the company in liquidation, in which case it would have gone forever, William Willson put it in the hands of a receiver to try and keep it going in the hope of finding a

Sir David Brown's 1969 Lagonda finally saw the light of production day in October 1974. With four doors and a conspicuously non-Aston grille it looked good and was actually a far nicer car than the few sales reflected.

buyer in more favourable times. Viewed as a three-year period in the long and chequered life of Aston Martin, it was one of achievement with a twice revised Aston continuing the line of development from the DB period, new markets entered and the Lagonda introduced. And despite all the production hiccoughs they had produced some 720 cars. They did try.

The receiver shut down the factory but continued to run the service department which at least kept some life apparent in the area. First to respond to the silent plea for help was the Aston Martin Owners' Club; established in 1935 they had long been great enthusiasts of the marque and, unlike many other such afficionado groups, they were equally involved with the company's current products – and they still are. But the money required to buy the company and give it sufficient capital injection to stand a chance of continuing was just too great.

In the economic climate of Great Britain at the time there wasn't much hope of finding a large English company to take Aston Martin

At the end of 1974 Company Developments put Aston Martin into receivership and made the entire workforce redundant. Here Fred Hartley is interviewed by David Dimbleby over the closure in January 1975.

Rex Woodgate was a tireless Aston Martin supporter in America and was largely responsible for introducing transatlantic interests to the 1975 purchase.

under its wing. But in America, Rex Woodgate, thwarted once again at the last moment in his efforts to sell Aston Martins, was trying hard to find potential owners among the generally wealthier Aston enthusiasts on his side of the Atlantic. Two who gleaned their background from Rex were Canadian restaurateur and sports car importer George Minden and former war correspondent, then boss of National Semi-

Conductors, the American, Peter Sprague. Both were still in their thirties, both were running very successful business groups and both were Aston enthusiasts – they liked other cars too but even now they still own Aston Martins. From across the Atlantic they approached from different directions, visited Newport Pagnell and then met in the Dorchester hotel, where both were staying.

Peter Sprague had the entrepreneurial mind that could more than cope with the financial side; George Minden was the engineer with a marketing flair who knew what made good cars good. They joined forces and on June 27th, paid £1,050,000 to the receiver, who, ably assisted by former Sales Manager Fred Hartley, had begun to put together some of the cars in process of build when the big shut-down came. There had been another potential contributor to the purchase, an Englishman, but he had finally failed to join the team. Meanwhile another English Aston fancier had also been to see the factory, unlit and unheated, the dust settling on the tools that had been left beside the now equally dusty part-built cars; even now, walking round the factory when all have gone home, I can imagine the Mary-Celeste-like scene that must have greeted those potential purchasers just ten years ago.

That second Aston fancier was Alan Curtis who, on one of his visits early in 1975, put a cross in the dust of a half-finished bonnet to denote the car that he would buy from the receiver. Alan had something of the entrepreneurial character of Peter Sprague, but he was involved in property and had a passion for flying. Despite the climate he was eventually prepared to put up just over £½ million to buy the company. However Sprague and Minden got there first and Alan was set to retire gracefully. It was only six weeks later that Peter Sprague talked him into replacing their original English partner. Six weeks after that the fourth member joined them; Denis Flather. He had retired from the family steel company in Sheffield and had left a cheque with the receiver against the possibility of becoming involved should the company ever restart.

Aston Martin Lagonda (1975) was in business.

Chapter Ten

Transfusion

At least the company thought it was in business. Fred Hartley assumed the role of Managing Director and quickly gathered together as many of the workforce as were initially required. Many had found other jobs, but the lure of Aston Martin was such that they soon gave notice to return to Newport Pagnell. On the engineering side Harold Beach stayed on as a consultant but the head became Mike Loasby, returning after a five year gap to find many of his former colleagues still around him.

Picking up the threads of production after a six-month gap was not as simple as might have been hoped. Some of the key suppliers were loathe to get involved again having lost money at the time of the receivership, while others had finally made obsolete the parts that perhaps only Aston had been using at the shut-down. An inevitable adjunct to a long model life for small volumes is that the parts that you can 'borrow' from other manufacturers became scarce and/or expensive when that manufacturer changes his model. Thus a number of components had to be re-sourced, retested or redesigned; initial production in the early days of the take-over was merely assembly of components on the line, including two more Lagondas.

It wasn't until the early part of 1976 that production could really be said to have restarted. By that time all the dealers required fresh contracts although most had remained self-retained service dealers, while the American operation never closed.

In March 1976 I visited the factory to see the first complete products of the new company roll off the line. Bearing in mind that the production process currently takes some 12 weeks for the Astons, March was the earliest to see a complete new car after a January start.

Employees had been gradually added to the various areas as the cars filtered through. It was certainly evident that some re-engineering had taken place in tidying up a chassis that was still very much stretched DB4.

One of the facts from George Minden's guided tour was that the bought out parts and material for a V-8 cost £5500 before the factory started adding value; that the car was priced at £13,631 including tax against the 1974 £11,349 shows a measure of the 1975 inflation but equally some evidence of the extent of the labour content.

I was told that the Lagonda, at that time just an Aston chassis cut and stretched in the sheet metal shop, would soon be having its own jigs. Despite a quoted price tag of £16,731 that Lagonda was, even then, never going to happen; they had already started on the striking Towns-styled car that we have today.

The new owners were unable to get production going again until January 1976. Indistinguishable from the previous company's, there was little need to change a car that the company expected to replace in a year or two.

Much of the engineering effort of 1976 was concentrated on the Lagonda first shown in October 1976, an incredibly rapid development time; here George Minden (left) and Peter Sprague look at their new car at its Aston Clinton launch.

While that is arguably outside the scope of this book, it cannot escape entirely as it had a profound effect on the fortunes of the company as the necessary support to the Aston V-8.

While V-8 production had been getting under way, some of the engineering time had been spent in providing a consultancy service – shades of Tickford to come – to the all but stillborn Bricklin sports car, while the factory had also made parts for a British stunt plane built in association with Cranfield – very much a function of the Alan Curtis flying interest.

By the end of 1975 the V-8 shape had nominally been around for eight years. William Towns was called in to produce styling studies for its replacement and for a Lagonda version. In January he was asked to produce a ⅜-scale clay model for the V-8; this he achieved by the end of the month. Minds were changed; would he now do one for the Lagonda four-door version instead – this was completed by the end of February. The go-ahead was agreed with the impossibly short pro-ramme to have the car on show at Earls Court that October, with production envisaged to start a year later. In fact the first part was achieved but production preparation took a further year of prolonged work; they started a slow pilot build in mid 1977 and the first two were used as cars for Motorfair that year. The third car followed being built up by the end of 1977

While the new car was inevitably styled around Aston components it was agreed by the management team before a functional interior and

American promotion for the new Lagonda with Rex Woodgate (left), Peter Sprague (centre) and Alan Curtis in good humour.

component mock-up had been laid out. The result was that it was designed from the outside in, which places a premium on ingenuity to find space for finite elements; that the engineers succeeded not only in fitting everything in, but also in designing a new air conditioning system and building a complete car in such a short period, shows the strength of support which the new owners enjoyed.

The shape of the new car was certainly futuristic but more so was the new instrumentation and switchgear; this was Mike Loasby's hobby-horse and inevitably found great favour with Peter Sprague. It had been developed in association with Cranfield but sadly was vastly over-complicated in its wiring and general circuitry.

I drove the second development car AML 1 early in 1978. At that stage the outside world were well aware of the Lagonda but had begun to regard it as a dream car that would never be fulfilled. When originally shown to the press in dummy cockpit form all the door switchgear was in the form of touch sensitive areas on an unmarked black panel. Fortunately these disappeared early on, and AML 1 had door switches

Show piece at the 1977 Auto Expo in Los Angeles, the first Lagonda is now in the National Motor Museum at Beaulieu.

Advanced instrumentation still in prototype form; Mike Loasby demonstrates.

that were very close to those that went into production; driver's door had little insert circles for touch operation controlling seat position and windows. Air conditioning controls were in the centre console. Each side of the single-spoke wheel were rectangular switch binnacles with touch circles both on their top face and the vertical face pointing towards the driver. The latter included touch controls for gear selection and for indicators. The whole was in a neat full width shallow facia. I can't say it was easy to get used to but it was unique and I felt it would be learnable. I enjoyed the rest of the car and finished my *Classic Car* article by saying: 'the Lagonda is not a gimmick looking for someone to impress, it is a serious super barouche'. It seemed ready for sale.

Following the successful crash test at MIRA on March 13th, 1978 the day finally came on April 24th for the ceremonial handing over of the first Lagonda to new director Lady Tavistock. Sadly that saw the company suffer one of the most embarrassing launches in the history of the motor industry. With the assembled press standing by to applaud, the car was pushed to the handover ceremony. Cranfield was still working on the computer and it was too late to install it. It was evident that the car was quite obviously not a production feasibility.

167

One who responded to that very public dilemma was Brian Refoy, President of Javelina Corporation in Dallas, Texas, a small electronics company which had begun to introduce digital instruments for the aftermarket in America. He started by rectifying the Tavistock car using some of his own instruments and then volunteered to provide his own systems for both instruments and switchgear. By that time jigs and tooling for chassis and those panels that weren't being produced by Superform were nearly completed; production was poised. In the middle of May Refoy produced his specification. AML was to ship out Lagonda 6 a month later and the first Javelina prototype would be with AML before the end of September. From the time of prototype approval, production units would follow ten weeks later. This was grasped and agreed.

At the time when the original launch target of Lagonda production in autumn 1977 was still believed attainable, thoughts had turned to the

The first production Lagonda (13008) was delivered twice to Lady Tavistock with a major instrumentation revision in between.

Federal specification V-8 with collapsing bumpers moved the indicators into the grille; repeater lights are on front and rear wings, while headlamps have the optional wipers.

Facia revision to the 1977 V-8 included lettered warning lights.

creation of a mid-engined Super Aston. This was Bulldog. When he had completed the clays for the Lagonda, William Towns started on a new striking wedge design for a practical two-seater; Towns was to complete his styling work by the end of that year and Mike Loasby was to work on the interior and chassis. With all the work on the Lagonda, progress on Bulldog was slow and, in 1977, the owners decided that Bulldog should be built away from the factory with all costs carried through one of Alan Curtis' other companies. It was planned to be launched at the 1978 Motor Show as a driveable concept car; it would have gullwing doors which reached 6ft 3in at their highest point for easy access over the well inset chassis side rails, there would be plenty of luggage space each side of the engine against the rear bulkhead, and visibility would be good with glass all round the cockpit.

In fact the car in half completed form got as far as the factory by October 1978, but at that point Loasby left to go to Delorean, so work ceased for a period. Steve Coughlin had arrived in 1977 from British Aerospace and had taken over from Loasby when he was seconded solely to the Bulldog project. It was Coughlin who reinstated the old DP system which had been dropped after the David Brown period. Thus DP1000 started the process again in 1979.

With the acceptance of the Lagonda came a renewed commitment to the V-8, which had been the company's only product. After the delayed restart some 207 cars had been sold during 1976 of which 83 had been in the UK, 73 in USA with the balance in the rest of the world. The first extension of the range came in February 1977 with the introduction of a high performance Vantage model; with revised cam-shafts and exhaust system, new 481DF Weber carburetters and bigger inlet valves it gave a claimed 40 per cent power increase in Aston's usual non-power-quoting terms. In fact the standard output by the end of 1976 was some 280bhp when running to the European emission standards; for the Vantage this was increased to 370bhp or 32 per cent – or 40 to the next round number. The standard V-8 benefited too, albeit with the same carburetters as before, with an increase to 304bhp.

With the Vantage came aerodynamic improvements; the grille was blanked off so that all cooling air came in under the bumper, a deep spoiler was added and the boot lid received a lip. Additionally its suspension was stiffened, Koni dampers were fitted and Pirelli's CN12s

Although the factory weren't really racing they tried the new 370bhp Vantage engine at the 1976 AMOC Silverstone with Mike Loasby at the helm. Blanked off grille and intake, deep spoiler and a tail lip spoiler were external features to distinguish the return of the true Vantage – this is V1.

were fitted on 7-inch rims; at £19,999 it was £3400 more than the V-8. Maximum speed was quoted as 168mph with a 0-60mph time of 5.4 seconds and 0-100mph in 13.0 seconds. A comparison with the 1973 V-8 which gave 5.7 and 13.6 seconds for 0-60 and 100mph reflects the effects of the additional weight of refinement and the loss of power in the standard car through lower emission levels.

I caught up with the Vantage shortly after its introduction in a *Supercar* comparison test. Accepting that it was impossible logistically to get a Lamborghini Countach, a Ferrari Boxer, a Porsche Turbo, a Maserati Khamsin, a Vantage and a Jaguar XJS all delivered at the same time for a week's comparative testing, I used the XJS for everyday comparison and borrowed each of the others on consecutive days, taking them all to the same carefully marked location for a composite photograph to be assembled later. At that time I didn't know Aston Martin power figures and was assuming 415bhp which, on 168mph, gave a rather brick-like drag factor of 0.46 – the worst of a group for

Once more the Volante; Harold Beach styled the new open top V-8 into an ageless shape which is still very popular. Wooden door cappings and instrument surround wood were introduced first on the Volante.

which the best, by calculation, was the Ferrari at 0.38. Using 370bhp for 168mph gives a fairer 0.41; by the time you allow for the fact that 168mph was over the power peak and consider the effects of the full production set-up of alternator, power steering pump and in-car exhaust system it is easy to accept the 0.384 drag factor achieved in 1971 testing as representative of today's Vantage.

In fact a production Vantage gives nearer 360bhp on the production test-bed, but these are taken after just three hours running in. After the equivalent of some 5000 miles, 375-380bhp is the norm.

Reverting though to the *Supercar* comparison. The Aston certainly scored well for its comfort, the quiet refinement at high cruising speeds with good road shock absorption matching the Jaguar surprisingly well, despite its generally firmer feel. Ferrari and Lamborghini were obviously good in performance and roadholding while the Porsche was almost as good but had the added practicality of two small seats in the rear – all I needed at the time. I plumped for the Porsche Turbo, then the same price as the Vantage, as the best mixture of enjoyment and practicality for everyday use; with a larger family I now appreciate the Aston Vantage for what it really is – the fastest supercar for the family man.

Despite all this activity on V-8s, Lagonda and Bulldog there was still time to respond to a further marketing request – the convertible Volante, another name reconjured from the DB period. When the company re-established its American dealership network in 1976, they were soon asking for a convertible version. Harold Beach drew one towards the end of that year, detailing the hood mechanisms and the shape of hood material and aluminium panelling that are with us today. In mid-1977 the go-ahead was given to design for production.

At that time there were fears that the convertible only had a short future ahead of it in America; laws were expected in 1981 to govern the height of the seat belt mountings, roll-over tests and the introduction of passive restraint systems, or airbags. These of course totally upset the design of the Triumph TR7 which appeared as a hard top only until the legislation was deferred, by which time it was too late for the TR7, but not for the Volante.

At Aston Martin the opportunity was grasped and the car was introduced in June 1978 with few problems on the way, other than convincing the authorities that the additional strengthening added precluded the need for either front or rear crash tests; given adequate supporting evidence the Department of Transport has it in its power to accept or reject them; equally American safety laws (as opposed to emission levels) are self-certifying – as long as the factory is happy, these are accepted, but woe betide anyone without adequate evidence if they get involved in any legal action after an accident. In fact the Volante was some 15 per cent stiffer in torsion than the V-8, although the bending stiffness was a little lower but there was no fear that the Volante was not as safe for occupants in a crash as in a V-8. Harold Beach quietly retired before the launch of his final offering – he had made a tremendous contribution during his 28 years.

In sales terms the Volante was an instant success. America took all of the 1978 production and the home market had to wait for their 37 units following the car's first show appearance. Overall production in 1978 peaked at over 300 cars, or 7 cars a working week, of which the V-8 accounted for 75 per cent, Vantage and Volante being equally split.

At the shareholder level, George Minden left the board in August 1978 at which time the company was making a modest profit. This left Peter Sprague and Alan Curtis as the major investors with Denis Flather still very much involved; it was Denis Flather who at this time tried to convince the rest of the board that his special automatic Vantage should be put into production. Eventually it was ruled out on several grounds, notably development costs to be covered by relatively few sales, high temperatures and safety with all that power.

The following year saw Bulldog return to life with the project handed to Keith Martin by Steve Coughlin who had taken over from Mike Loasby. Martin set up a special area at the far end of the service department, cordoned off from the main engineering workshop. With a small team he took over the collection of parts and turned it into reality during the ensuing twelve months; it was first shown to the press in April 1980 by which time the engine had grown twin turbochargers. It had lost its beam axled front end, and was capable of 200mph, although that was never given the chance to be proven – 191mph was the best ever seen at MIRA which is a very short track indeed at those speeds.

Otherwise 1979 was generally bad news; it was the start of the

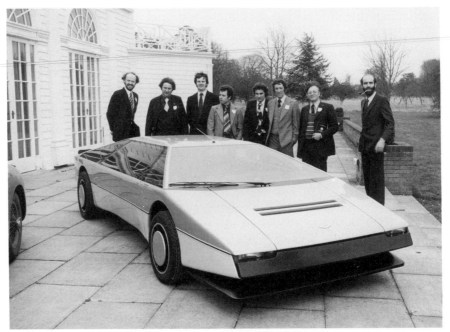

The mid-engined Bulldog returned to development life as the flagship of Aston Martin's external engineering facility. It was shown at Aston Clinton surrounded by its team of creators. From left: Steve Hallam, John Caesar, Steve Coughlin, Jim Corrie, Bob Clarke, Pete Collins, Mike Duff, Keith Martin. Digital instrumentation used LCD; it was fully trimmed as a driveable concept car.

depression, interest rates were rising world-wide and output was savagely hacked back by 100 cars. The Lagonda was barely on stream and the fort was held by the V-8 and Volante at 90-odd cars each with 20 Vantages, mostly for the UK. There were inevitable redundancies by the end of the year. America fared worse with 50 orders of 1978 dropping to a mere 21, all Volantes. National Semi-Conductors were having a lean time, reducing Peter Sprague's major source of income; Alan Curtis had to take over the bank guarantees, and, at higher interest rates, the modest profit that Aston had recorded in 1978, turned the other way.

But 1979 wasn't all bleak. October 1978 had seen the launch of the latest series of V-8, the Oscar India body-style with such interior changes as a revised air-conditioning, wooden facia and a host of minor details. In fact work had started on this as the Vantage had been introduced, and William Towns was once again consultant on the

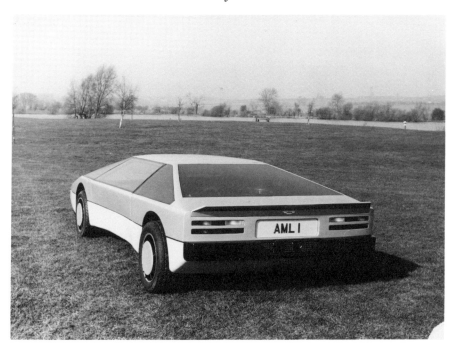

With the AMOC Silverstone meeting again used as a test track, this Vantage (V2) was driven by Ray Mallock and David Morgan. It was the prototype of the revised bodyshape; the bonnet bulge has no intake and it was extended to the rear edge of the bonnet to hide the wiper spindles. The waistline strip was not carried into production.

revised tail treatment and modified bonnet bulge – tea-tray spoilers for V-8 and Vantage – and the interior. The price had now gone to £23,000 for the V-8 and £26,000 for the Vantage while the Volante, which wasn't delivered in the UK until March 1979 was a resounding £33,864.

I first drove the Volante in May 1979 and loved it. It is interesting now to see from old internal memos that we nearly didn't get our *Thoroughbred and Classic Cars* test vehicle as the Engineering Department had greater need of it for further stiffening of the rear end to reduce chassis shake; a steel reinforcing structure had to be added in the middle of that year. It was all that an Aston had become with the refinement of the saloon unimpaired; with its double-lined hood raised it was difficult to tell that you weren't in a saloon. The boot was smaller than that of the saloon which made one appreciate the fitted luggage, and the rear seat space had likewise suffered a little due to the need to accommodate the collapsed hood, but it was, and is, a timeless and elegant creation.

Not satisfied though with the Oscar India changes of 1978, the company introduced further changes for the 1979 show. Outwardly these were further detail enhancement with central locking doors, rear fog lights, bonnet gas struts, seat release changes, rear screen timer and several more. But prospects for the end of the recession were still unpredictable; Aston Martin Lagonda was going to have to look for other ways of generating the cash to support the group.

By mid-1980 plans had hardened. AML would offer the services of its engineers to the motor industry at large, and Bulldog would be the flagship for the prototype to production facility of Aston Martin Tickford – the old coachbuilding name acquired by David Brown in 1955 was once again serving a useful purpose. Meanwhile moves had been afoot to take the company into the realms of mass production through the acquisition of the declining MG subsidiary of British Leyland who wished to close the Abingdon factory. Alan Curtis had spearheaded the formation of a consortium which was also to include Toyota from Japan; it got so close to happening during 1980 that many believed it had happened both inside the company and out. Work had been virtually completed on a revised MGB while investigation had taken place on its potential replacement.

Further changes to the engine came in June 1980 in an attempt to ease production variations which had proliferated with various markets and models. The basic engine became a cross between the torquey Lagonda and the Vantage; this gave polynomial cams, bigger inlet valves and ports, reduced overlap and a 9.3:1 compression ratio using the Vantage pistons with valve pockets and barrel shaped skirts; Lagondas require squatter inlet manifolds for bonnet clearance while Federal versions of both have the pistons machined to a lower compression, 8.0:1, to meet the latest Federal NOx requirements following a 1980 reduction.

For all models, smaller ports were introduced, with higher lift overlap cam timing for the Vantage. In practice these changes made very little difference to the overall power output but improved the torque and fuel consumption on all models. Fuel consumption was further improved on

Extended use of leather with the Volante wood characterised the new model which was launched in October 1978. BTM 780T is the second of Denis Flather's automatic transmission Vantages; these were never offered as a production car as the Vantage torque leaves the Chrysler Torque-flite with little safety margin.

automatic transmission cars with the use of the lock-up torque converter which takes the slip out of the fluid drive in top gear once the torque conversion has finished.

Thus the start of 1980 appeared to be promising, but by then the UK market had dwindled to less than half its 1979 level and Lagondas were the greatest seller with 33 out of the 74 total. Sales in 1980 overall were down to just 150 cars; fortunately America was still in love with the Volante, taking 39 that year.

On the general engineering front further work had been undertaken on turbocharging with a twin-turbo installation in one of the development Lagondas. It was felt that this was a possible route to give increased performance within emission limitations and the unit developed some 370bhp. Parallel work on the Bulldog unit had seen up to 735bhp which was felt to be a promising basis for a marine version – sadly still-born due to lack of outside funds.

Work had been carried out on another engine too, the Weslake V-12.

While Aston Martin had a fair number of development engineers they no longer had an engine designer; so in 1979 they took on Alastair Lyle from Cosworth. This addition was invaluable for his input into the tubocharging work to start with, but the real purpose was to start work on the next generation Aston engine. Despite the renewed commitment to the V-8, it was obviously recalled that it had taken six years to get the V-8 from the drawing board into production.

Favoured configuration at the time was a V-12 for its smooth power delivery. It happened that Weslake was closing down just at this time and there was a working V-12 up for sale. This had started life as the power unit for Dan Gurney's formula one car; in its sole season of 1967, it gave Gurney victory in the Race of Champions and at the very fast Belgian Grand Prix at Spa. The Gurney association had stemmed from the Gurney-Weslake heads designed for the GT40s; John Wyer's Gulf team had considered the Weslake V-12 in 1967 for the Mirage when it was producing a claimed 417bhp as the desirable Cosworth DFV had been assigned to Len Bailey's F3L project.

Anticipating the eventual take-over of MG, Aston Martin restyled the MGB with wrap-round bumpers, two-tone anti-chip paintwork and new alloy wheels.

At that time the V-12 was regarded as unproven for long distance racing so the idea was dropped in favour of the BRM V-12 used briefly in the 1969 Mirage M2. However by the time that endurance racing had been reduced to 3-litres in 1973, the Cosworth was proving equally troublesome with vibration problems. Ford decided to back this both ways by leaving the Cosworth to the Grand Prix world and taking over Weslake's second generation V-12 to offer the Gulf team for 1973; by now John Wyer was more of a consultant to the team which was headed by his former assistant, John Horsman.

The engine's sole appearance was at the 1973 Le Mans test weekend where it was installed in one of the earlier chassis clothed in a new low-drag coupé body designed by Len Bailey. The car failed to prove its worth, suffering from fuel feed problems and the car never reappeared in that form, neither body nor engine being used again. Weslake continued development on it though and it had apparently yielded 490bhp.

For 1980 Vantage, V-8 and Lagonda specifications were integrated with torque improvements all-round and better fuel economy. This is Victor Gauntlett's car which Motor *road-tested estimating the maximum speed at 168mph, reaching 60mph in 5.2 seconds and 100mph in 11.9 seconds.*

Lagonda 13004 was used as a test-bed for a turbocharging installation with the sealed American airbox. It was impressively fast.

Thus, bearing in mind that the V-8 had been designed for racing to be detuned for the road, the V-12 seemed a promising project and AML took over all the parts, drawings, patterns and complete design rights. It was hoped that it would stand a stretch to 4-litres. Thus DP1080 – referred to as the 1985 engine – was opened in late 1979. Over the next few months it readily became apparent that the claimed figures were not true steady state outputs and that torque was inadequate. While Weslake's theories had stood him in very good stead for the 1930-70 period where increasing port air-flow always seemed to produce more power than did the original standard engine, seventies technology had found better ways of creating power with torque. The V-12's ports were far too large and it was going to need a lot of other redesigning to get it into a useable production unit even in 3.4-litre form which was felt to be the maximum it could take. First figures showed 380bhp at 9500rpm; although work continued on trying to improve this the project was finally cancelled in the second half of 1980.

Mock-up of the proposed turbocharged marine version of the V-8 which sadly was never taken up due to lack of finance.

However 1980 was significant in other ways; three new shareholders joined the ranks. Peter Cadbury arrived in January then CH Industrials and Pace Petroleum joined in May; under Chairman Tim Hearley, CHI had a particular interest in the MG project as they were original equipment suppliers of the soft top components, CH standing for Coventry Hood. Pace Petroleum had been founded in 1972 as an independent petrol supplier to the smaller garage as well as to industrial users. By 1980 the company had 400 outlets and was doing well. Both Gauntlett and Curtis lived in Farnham, Surrey, sharing an interest in flying as well as in worthwhile motorcars.

By the end of 1980 despite the extra financial injection, the poor state of the market had taken its toll, and AML had supported a continuously high level of engineering development on a wide range of projects. Alan Curtis, who had taken over as virtually resident managing director in 1977, was bearing the major brunt. The only way ahead appeared to be to cut production right down to the level of a car a week, keep the service side going and develop the south side of Tickford. This found little favour with Tim Hearley or Victor Gauntlett, who couldn't see Aston Martin surviving without a production facility ensuring the continuity of the name in the public eye. Accordingly Pace and CHI agreed to buy out the existing shareholders at the end of 1980 and Aston Martin Lagonda (1975) Limited became just Aston Martin Lagonda Limited. Peter Cadbury sold his shares to the new owners shortly afterwards and Denis Flather resigned a little later.

The five years of AML (1975) can be recalled with satisfaction by those involved. A lot happened. The Lagonda was designed and put into production, the Volante was launched, Vantage had returned, the V-8s were further refined and Bulldog had arrived to herald the birth of Aston's external engineering service. Given a continuation of the 1978 production level the Curtis team might well have continued, but once again external forces prevailed.

Chapter Eleven

Refinement

The new owners moved in over the new year period at the beginning of 1981. Victor Gauntlett would be Chief Executive and joint Chairman with Tim Hearley; CHI Managing Director John Kinder also joined the board while the Managing Director from Pressed Steel Fisher was John Symonds who had joined AML in October 1979. CHI was a public company also involved in property, and was to move into other motor industry areas to replace their loss of hood sales. With Pace Petroleum appearing self-supporting, Gauntlett was able to spend the middle three days of the week at Aston Martin, or at least working for Astons, because he soon turned his natural talents for salesmanship to the marketing side and embarked on a series of tours to the Middle and Far East and to America.

At this time the Middle East was reaping the benefits of its spiral of petroleum price increases and had the wherewithal to appreciate the craftsmanship and fine qualities of the Lagonda, which almost sold on looks alone in the Arab market. So 1981 saw them take nearly 50 units of which 75 per cent were Lagondas.

Experience in oil industry negotiations with the Middle East had taught Victor Gauntlett that it was a volatile market which couldn't be guaranteed to last. The US was obviously the market of the future, but the Lagonda was still 18 months away in Federal form with a further NOx reduction in 1981.

When Sprague, Minden and Curtis had taken over, they had moved the import facility to New Rochelle on the North East outskirts of New York. Rex Woodgate came back to the factory and Sprague's protégé, Maurice Hallowell, took over. The new owners, though, felt that their American centre of operations should have its own dealership as a base

Victor Gauntlett moved in as Joint Chairman and Chief Executive in January 1981 retaining his chairmanship of his own Pace Petroleum. A lover of fast cars he sees the Aston Martin as the true successor to the products of W. O. Bentley.

and moved this to Greenwich, Connecticut, taking over the old site of Luigi Chinetti's Ferrari centre, an attractive half-timbered, wooden-panelled building remarkably redolent of old England.

While the American market had taken all but 10 out of the 48 Volantes sold in 1980, the 1981 sales had declined by ten units, but included half a dozen V-8s. It was to be well worth sustaining against the future decline of the Middle East and the Lagonda arrival.

By now the V-8 in all its forms had reached a level of refinement that was difficult to improve significantly, and effort was concentrated on maintaining the quality. It has to be realised that the car was essentially nearly 15 years old; many of the original components which had been shared by other manufacturers were now only required by Aston Martin; in some cases this meant a supplier price increase but at worst the stoppage of that component. Thus much of the engineering was, and is, devoted to finding fresh suppliers, adapting their products and retesting. The days when suppliers were keen to be associated with a prestige company had begun to diminish in favour of purely commerical considerations.

By the end of 1981, overall sales had improved to an extra 25 units over 1980 but this was more than accounted for by the Middle East demand which was 45 units higher than the previous year; the recession was beginning to bite at home and demand for the V-8 and Lagonda had halved although Vantage and Volante held their 1980 figures. Doubtless some of that was due to the *Motor* road test of the Vantage – it was the fastest standard production car they had ever tested, regardless of the fact that it was still a four-seater, and the report was full of superlatives.

The engineering division's launch into the motor industry was looking promising; while some of the early associations failed to reach fruition, others succeeded – notably the Lancia Hi-Fi, the Frazer Tickford Metro and the development of the endurance racing engine for the new Nimrod Racing team which will be covered in the final chapter. The Tickford Capri was to follow; this started from initial work performed by John Miles, the former GP driver and *Autocar* journalist, on the suspension of his own Capri which then became part of a package agreed by Ford's Bob Lutz and Victor Gauntlett, whereby Tickford would develop a complete mini Aston with turbocharging and

Tim Hearley was the other Joint Chairman who retained his chairmanship of the public company C H Industrials, founded in the Motor Industry as the Coventry Hood and Sidescreen Company.

First car to bear the name of the new Tickford was the Frazer Tickford Metro with Simon Saunders' styling bolt-ons, luxury interior and uprated A-series engine.

revised bodywork for Ford to market. Gauntlett and Jaguar's John Egan signed a contract for Tickford to develop an XJS cabriolet – at that time a remarkable piece of bridge-building between Astons and British Leyland still smarting under the failed MG takeover.

In the latter part of 1981 Aston Martin Tickford was established as a separate company working for Aston Martin on a preferential hourly rate. In hindsight this perhaps slowed Aston Martin work to some extent, in that every hour became costed, something that had never before happened within Aston Martin's own engineering department.

The essential work of getting the Lagonda into America continued as a matter of urgency. By this time considerable experience had been gained with the Lagonda and the time was ripe to start on changes; most notable of these were to introduce dropping rear side windows – thought unnecessary with air conditioning – fitting a rear air conditioning unit as standard and removing the door-mounted seat and window switches to the centre console. Work proceeded on these and other

Next on the Tickford scene was the Tickford Capri with similar styling theme to that of the Metro, but included a totally revised suspension package and an effective turbocharger installation.

Tickford's biggest break came with a contract to develop the XJS Cabriolet and then to put it into production at CHI's Bedworth factory near Coventry.

detail improvements during 1982, when the car was introduced to the American market, and on through 1983 when the full Mk. II package was introduced for all markets.

For the V-8, revised air conditioning controls and more interior woodwork were part of the 1983 update which also included the adoption of BBS wheels with an 8-inch rim for the Vantage; this last was particularly important as Pirelli required unnaturally high pressures for their P7s on the narrower rim which adversely affected the ride quality – given an 8-inch rim including wider wheel arch flares the sub-130mph pressures came down to 28psi from 42psi.

On the sales front, the Middle East continued to be the mainstay during 1982 taking 61 Lagondas in their 74 imports, but overall production was down to a mere 160 cars; America took 36 including an instant 14 Lagondas following a successful October launch, but the home market sank to an all-time low of less than 30 cars, with the good old V-8 the major contributor at 10 units, Lagonda and Volante at 8 each.

In management circles, John Symonds had left in August 1981 while CHI supplied Bill Archer the following year to cover the production side.

1983 was to prove another crucial year for Aston Martin; down in Farnham, Pace was beginning to have a difficult time with slender margins consumed overnight during the savage price-cutting that was necessarily part and parcel of a market with an oil glut; Victor had to spend more time at the petroleum helm and control at Newport Pagnell gradually shifted to the CHI side – Bill Archer took on the task of Managing Director but the group was still owned 50/50 by Pace and CHI.

Faced with a world petroleum glut of their own making, the Middle East had less to spend in the West, and Victor Gauntlett was no longer as available to add his own brand of salesmanship to that of Colin Thew; their demand dropped to less than 40 per cent of the previous year at just 28 cars, 25 of them Lagondas.

Unfortunately Aston Martin wasn't really in a position to respond; there was industrial unrest within the workforce over bonus schemes. While Bill Archer brought in much that was good with in-house systems, his response to a prolonged period of confrontation was to dismiss the panel-beaters. This all but brought the company to the ground.

At the same time Pace had begun to receive overtures for a take-over, a probable condition being recovery of the investment in Aston Martin. CHI were aware of this and equally aware that the chances of new partners arriving on the scene were pretty slim with an idle factory.

A rapid back-track saw Bill Archer resign in July 1983 and Victor Gauntlett return to the daily helm, getting production going again, although the year's sales were to sink to an all-time low of just 134 cars.

At the American importership Peter Sprague held the nominal share that he had retained from 1980, but a small shareholding had been bought by Peter Livanos of the well known Greek shipping family. Peter had come in to buy a second hand Aston at New Rochelle – his uncle had been an Aston owner – and decided to join the fold; it was he who introduced the move to Greenwich. He had been involved in the early

The current Aston range shows off its new BBS wheels which allowed the Vantage to adopt 8-inch rims. Although basically a 1967 bodyshape still, the V-8 has moved from modern to classic appeal without a pause for obsolescence.

Victor Gauntlett with Aston Martin, Pace tanker and a carefully stacked array of Pace oil.

days of the Nimrod project. A subsequent fundraising shuffle saw Livanos and shipping broker Nicholas Papanicolaou (owner with his brother John, of London – and American-based Titan Shipping Brokerage) take a majority shareholding in Aston Martin Lagonda of North America Inc through a separate company created for the purpose, called Automotive Investments Incorporated. This was then followed by the purchase by AII of the Pace Petroleum shares, adjusted slightly to give AII 55 per cent of the Aston Martin Lagonda shareholding, but an equal stake in Aston Martin Tickford – CHI remained the other shareholder in both companies. However part of AII's agreement to purchase Pace's Aston shares was that Victor Gauntlett should run it full time on their behalf. This was obviously only possible if Victor sold Pace lock stock and barrel, and divorced himself from the industry he had known all his working life and the company he had created eleven years earlier.

While Pace had reached the stage of seeing the way ahead and being able to trade out of a difficult spell, there was no doubt that the takeover would ensure the future for company and employees and the return of the Aston capital would clinch the deal. In fact this looked like happening slightly ahead of the AII request that Victor run Astons, so there was a short spell when he could have stayed on to run Pace under new ownership – an unlikely prospect which would actually have suited neither party.

Thus in a very short period, Pace moved out of Aston, the Hays Group took over Pace and Victor Gauntlett returned to Aston Martin full-time. It was just one of life's little ironies that Hays is backed by the Kuwait Investment Trust and it was the Middle East market that had failed Astons that year. The actual sale of Pace to the Hays Group was only finalised in September.

While a simple check of sales over the near three years of Pace involvement might present a steady decline, there is equally no doubt that the decline would have been greater had it not been for the Gauntlett influence and the Pace contributions. Pace single-handedly covered Aston's promotional activities for three years which led many to believe that Aston Martin was part of Pace Petroleum Group. Pace sponsored Aston's involvement in the Dubai Grand Prix of 1981; they sponsored the Aston Martin Owners' Club activities for three years; they took Aston Martin back into racing, to name but a few involvements that helped to promote the Aston name. Costly it may have been, but the benefit was mutual for Pace and Aston; inevitably it played down CHI's co-ownership at the time, but it also saved them a great deal of expense.

From the start AII and CHI were uneasy partners and it wasn't long before AII exercised a built-in option to purchase the balance of shares in Aston Martin Lagonda in exchange for a controlling interest in Aston

Pace Petroleum sponsored the Aston participation in the December 1981 Dubai GP with Bulldog leading Vantage and Lagonda.

The Aston parade gets under way at Dubai with Viscount Downe's Project 212 and DBR1 at the head of the older cars.

Martin Tickford with the balance held by Aston Martin Lagonda, not AII. So in April 1984 Aston Martin Lagonda Limited once more became wholly owned by trans-atlantic interests, who also owned the importership of the company's major market. At the same time Aston

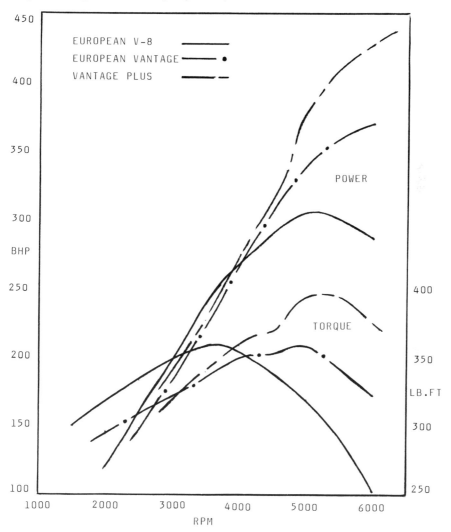

First of the new DP regime was DP2000 to develop a higher performance version of the Vantage, as an option for markets that do not require type approval or for others as an after-market fitment. With raised compression, higher lift cams, bored out carburetters and big bore exhaust this unit develops 437bhp at 6200rpm with a higher torque than the standard Vantage. Vantage develops 370bhp while V-8 has a still healthy 305bhp.

lost their own engineering facility. Much of the equipment and many of the engineering staff moved out to the new CHI facility in nearby Milton Keynes, willing and able to continue development work for Aston Martin on a commercial basis along with the rest of the motor industry.

Tickford were by now established as engineering consultants and specialist coachbuilders; they were now producing the Jaguar XJS Cabriolet at the old Coventry Hood site in Bedworth, along with the Tickford Capri which had returned to them following a Ford cut-back. Race engine development too stayed with Tickford.

Unwilling to have to depend entirely on an outside company no longer on the premises for day-to-day engineering, AII sought to establish their own compact engineering group to cover that production assistance and further development of the existing cars, which is where the author came in having come from Pace in September 1983 to set up that group. Some of the Tickford employees decided to return to Aston Martin Lagonda, while more came from the outside motor industry to make an effective unit.

While all this was happening the sales were looking up. The home market leapt to a demand for 80 cars as those who had weathered the depression became less shy; the European mainland looks set for a 50 per cent increase with new dealers appointed in France and Germany; and in the USA, where Peter Gaydon had been installed as an AML employee to run the Greenwich importership in early 1983 there was a market for 100 units, half the latest Lagondas and half the ever-popular Volante.

Within the new engineering wing the major work was on new Lagonda instrumentation using three cathode ray tubes and a computer to monitor all the information previously displayed on the digital dashboard. Like the preceding system the development of this had been in the hands of Javelina for the previous five years; from January 1984 it had further development at Newport Pagnell and was ready to be launched at the 1984 Motor Show – the first car in production with a CRT display.

But not everything on the horizon was sunny.

Chapter Twelve

Return to Racing

While Aston Martin's final fling as a works team was successful with Project 214's win at Montlhery in 1963, the V-8 sortie with the Lola had been an unmitigated disaster. There was little enthusiasm for a racing return in the David Brown period once John Wyer had left; the Company Developments team was against such an idea from the start, but the Sprague/Minden/Curtis regime would have liked to have gone back to the circuits, given a suitable car. With the delay on Bulldog there wasn't even the basis of such a car.

Robin Hamilton was an Aston Martin dealer based at Fauld near Tutbury in the countrified outskirts of Burton on Trent; like many an Aston enthusiast he dreamed of taking Aston Martin back to Le Mans. A former Rolls Royce apprentice and amateur racer, he was also sufficient of an engineer to know what was required to convert a V-8 into something resembling a racing GT car during the winter of 1976/7. While Aston Martin weren't about to get involved as a company, they were keen to help where they could, and Mike Loasby put a certain amount of time into the car and engine development; some of that work could be seen in the 1977 Vantage. Hamilton's engine developed some 480bhp with Weber IDA carburetters and dry sump lubrication.

The first outing was at Silverstone for the 6-hour race in 1977 where Robin with David Preece co-driving failed to finish. However Le Mans a month later saw the car out with the addition of Mike Salmon; despite the relatively great weight of the car they finished seventeenth, failing to classify as they were part of the prototype category and did not cover the required distance.

Shortage of sponsorship prevented a return in 1978, but, by 1979, the car was fitted with twin turbochargers and the roofline had been

Robin Hamilton's first Le Mans sortie was in 1977 with this heavily modified Vantage; they finished outside classification in seventeenth place, but it was a good start.

lowered; it was a 'silhouette' Vantage but recognisably an Aston. At Silverstone, Hamilton with Preece and Derek Bell finished in thirteenth place but Le Mans saw the car suffering from a lack of brakes after 2½ hours and they retired. Although that car again appeared in 1980 Silverstone, Robin's mind was set on higher things; he was determined to take Aston Martin back to Le Mans with a car that stood a chance of performing well.

During the latter part of the seventies the World Championship of Makes had been reduced to a boring procession first of two-seater Grand Prix cars and then with variations on a Porsche 911 theme in 934/5/6 forms during 1980/1. For 1982 a new sports car formula was envisaged with 1000Kg cars using production-based engines. Aston Martin had the V-8 homologated in group 4, later in group B. It was an encouraging enough combination to start Robin on the trail of Nimrod; that the formula was subsequently changed to 800Kg cars with racing engines built by group B manufacturers, was at best unfortunate but, in reality a mistake by the organising body.

Determined to give an Aston-powered car a sound chance of being on the Le Mans grid in the first year of the new Group C, Hamilton approached Eric Broadley to produce a modernised version of the Lola Aston – the old combination with the technology of 1980. It was a calculated risk that the eventual Group C rules would conform closely to the then current IMSA rules.

By the time I saw the car in mid-1981 the first chassis was at Fauld, some wind-tunnel testing had been performed on a basic model and the car was taking shape around an Aston engine and a Hewland gearbox. Hamilton approached Victor Gauntlett on both the Pace sponsorship and Aston involvement fronts.

Before committing himself Victor had asked Aston engineers to assess the Hamilton car, a March chassis and an in-house possibility. While the Aston men were critical of the lack of the latest ground effect tunnels they were equally unable to build a car in-house for anything less than double the price.

Eventually Nimrod Racing Automobiles was formed with Hamilton, Gauntlett and Peter Livanos (from AMLNA Inc) as shareholders. On

First Nimrod seen at Hamilton's workshop in Fauld near Burton-on-Trent. The second chassis is nearing completion behind.

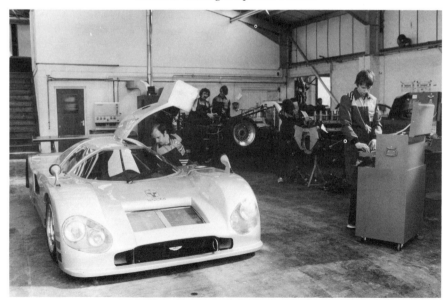

their own Aston Martin could not afford to be involved but Pace Petroleum could; the newly formed Aston Martin Tickford would prepare race engines on a purely commercial basis, first a carburetted 525bhp engine, later a 575bhp Lucas fuel injected version. All were convinced that the return of Aston Martin, however remotely, to the tracks would attract a worthwhile major sponser, and equally that there would be other buyers of the new car. Accordingly the order was given to lay down five chassis.

Against this background there was a grand launch in November 1981 at Goodwood. James Hunt and Stirling Moss drove the first car fitted with a Hamilton prepared 480bhp carburetter engine, Frank Bough hosted the reception and the world's press were in attendance. The car had been run at Silverstone prior to this with Derek Bell at the wheel and seemed to be heading in the right direction.

Car testing continued through November mostly at Silverstone where various drivers were tried; on the basis that more mature drivers are essential for long distance racing, in that they are not out to prove

Aston Martin Tickford developed the 5340cc V-8 to 525bhp with carburetters as an interim before the injection version with 575bhp. In this form the unit is unstressed when in the chassis (left). Stressed version for 1983 is shown for comparison.

their Grand Prix worthiness, Tiff Needell and Bob Evans were early choices, while at this stage it was reckoned that Daytona and Sebring would also be included, so Drake Olson became part of the team and spent much time at Fauld learning the cars from the inside out. Perhaps Hamilton did not select Ray Mallock, a former Aston employee and successful F2 driver, because he didn't want a conflict of engineering interests – Hamilton had his own ideas on developing a car and Ray would certainly have his. Geoff Lees, the 1981 F2 champion, joined the team during the winter.

By now the rules of Group C had been published, if not finalised, and there were sufficient differences between those and the American IMSA rules to preclude one design being suitable for both series and Daytona/Sebring were no longer in the Endurance Championship. With inadequate funding for two onslaughts and therefore no prospect of running in America, Peter Livanos was to drop out of the team early in 1982.

Nimrod's works driver line-up for 1982. From left, Bob Evans, Tiff Needell and Geoff Lees. Nimrod motif can be seen on the transporter.

205

During the first week in December 1981 there was the Dubai Grand Prix, Birmingham entrepreneur Martin Hone's Middle East extravaganza which was to include an Aston Martin grid and a number of other Aston flag-wavers to assist the launch of a Dubai dealership; three Lagondas, two Aston Bulldogs and a Nimrod were added to the 20 race cars. The whole was a most enjoyable exercise but, in Nimrod terms, the upshot was that Viscount Downe, whose DBRI and Project 212 were to finish first and second in the Aston race, decided to return to modern Endurance Racing and ordered the second Group C chassis, 004, as 003 was earmarked for the Nimrod team, 001 staying in IMSA trim. Lord Downe had raced ex-works DBRI and Project cars during the 1961/4 period and is the AMOC President. Richard Williams, the Brixton-based Aston specialist, looked after the DBRI and Project cars, so he would manage the Downe team, for which the drivers would be Mike Salmon, Ray Mallock and Simon Phillips, the latter two having

With both his ex-works Astons at Dubai, Viscount Downe decided to join the Nimrod fold when he saw it demonstrated by Derek Bell. Here Roy Salvadori in the Downe DBR1 leads David Preece in the ex-Ogier DB4GT and Roger Hart in the ex-Ogier Zagato.

driven Phillips's cars in previous Le Mans events.

Work now continued on the two Group C cars, but equally hard work was being expended on finding sponsorship for the team. Sadly, all avenues failed; despite the prospect of a full hour's TV film to come no-one came alongside. To retain the chance of offering a two-car team Victor Gauntlett put Pace sponsorship into the Downe team, the running of which was being underwritten by Simon Phillips.

Chassis 003 had its first run in February and gradually improved its Silverstone times to the upper 1 minute 25 seconds but this was some way off the expected target of 1 minute 20 seconds. Obviously the car was too heavy, but it was too late to do anything significant about that for 1982; aerodynamically it was not perfect but this was attainable with the usual splitters, spoilers and wings.

What had become more significant though, since the design had been laid down, was the arrival of ground effect theory for GP cars and the Nimrod simply didn't have any under-body tunnels; the original plans for group C had been to have a flat bottom – it turned out to be a flat area which still allowed some underbody reshaping ahead of, and behind, that flat area. While this was less important for Le Mans theory where maximum speed is a significant factor, it meant that the car was never going to be quick on the rest of the Endurance circuits.

Development was also being hampered by a spate of engine failures, eventually corrected by valve spring redesign and a recommendation to keep normal engine revs down to 6800rpm rather than the 7200rpm that Hamilton's men had been using. In their tests Tickford had motored valve gear at 8000rpm for 24 hours with no ill-effects so the problem took some time to trace.

The Downe team received their chassis in April, not long before the proposed first race at Silverstone on May 16th, an event sponsored by Pace, giving the Pace/Aston/Nimrod axis a superb platform. The Williams team immediately stripped the car and rebuilt it to incorporate all they had learnt from previous long distance experience, and then Ray Mallock started on the development. That he was slightly more effecive became apparent at the Silverstone race where 004's best time was 1 minute 24.88 seconds against Lees's best for 003 at 1 minute 25.33 seconds.

The Hamilton team was still having engine troubles but the Downe

Part of the promotional package to obtain sponsorship for the Nimrod team were these models built up by Bert Sloman, who did all the Nimrod glassfibre work and a bit of the shaping as well.

Line-up on Press day for the 1982 Pace Six Hour race at Silverstone. From left, 003 with Bob Evans/Geoff Lees, 004 with Robin Hamilton/Simon Phillips/Ray Mallock and 001 with Victor Gauntlett and Tiff Needell.

car was being restricted to 6500rpm and had no trouble. In the race 004 was set to start slow and run around the 1 minute 30 second mark, while 003 was to run at a comfortable speed for the drivers, Lees and Evans. Ickx had lapped the new Porsche 956 in 1 minute 16.91 seconds, over a second faster than the first Lancia which was running in the carry-over Group 6 form with no roof.

A further group C change had been that the top of the windscreen was also dictated rather than just overall height. The Nimrod screen was too low, so a strip of portholes had to be let into the roof to increase the nominal height of the transparent section; while this dodge was accepted at Silverstone, the team had to add taxi signs to the screen at Le Mans – unsightly drag increasers.

The Nimrods started well in their first race. By running through the first hour, Lees/Evans/Needell were actually in fifth place; 004 had stopped just before the hour but was up to sixth after two hours with 003 now eighth. At this stage in group C there was only one 956 but several 935 and 936, so the opposition was not as hot as it was to

003 grew a beard after practice for the 1982 Silverstone race. Port-hole strip can be seen in the roof centre.

become; Lancia had two works cars and Ford had only one C100, but Rondeau was also flying the Cosworth flag.

Group C's fuel allocation may have worked for distance races but trying to equate 6 hours with 1000km at Silverstone did not work because the cars were set to cover nearer 1150km, so the front end had to run slow to conserve fuel. 003's race was run when it stopped out on the circuit with apparent rotor arm failure after 148 laps – it was actually more serious. But 004 just kept going with a clockwork run and finished sixth, fourth in group C and well in the points. It was a very encouraging first outing, provided development could keep going at the same pace as the rivals.

Le Mans now loomed and Mallock continued development of 004 and managed to get his best Silverstone lap down to 1 minute 22.9 seconds using a revised front wishbone to reduce understeer among other adjustments. The engine programme now looked as if it had worked but the 004 team still kept their revs down.

Practice saw the Downe team just faster than 003 at 3 minutes 46.34 seconds against 3 minutes 48.17 seconds which qualified the cars in

Pit stop for 004 at Silverstone 1982 with Ray Mallock in the car; both cars bore Pace sponsorship.

Nimrod 003 at Le Mans 1982 before its accident; limited sponsorship came via Pioneer. Screen blister supplemented the roof portholes.

twenty-third and twenty-sixth places. Porsche led with 3 minutes 28.4 seconds. While Rondeau were to lead for the first three hours, and Ford C100 at four hours, it was a Porsche demonstration thereafter.

The works Nimrod team set off very quickly lapping as fast in the race as in practice, or faster since Lees's best was to be 3 minutes 46.0 seconds while the Downe team was more cautious with a 4-minute target. After three hours 003 had seen seventh place while 004 was around tenth, but, 40 minutes into the fourth hour, Needell had an almighty spin when flat out down the Mulsanne straight, cannoning off the Armco; heavy though the Nimrod was, it was also very safe; Needell was unscathed and the car recoverable. It is probable that a tyre blew out due to centrifugal growth causing it to hit the underside of the wheelarch, but almost as likely was a collapse of the rear bodywork onto the tyre.

004 soldiered on, picking up places through sheer reliability and at half distance they were up to an amazing fourth place behind three Porsches; some 32 cars had retired by then. By 8 o'clock on the Sunday

morning they were still fifth but at 10.30 am the car came in with a misfire; while this was eventually traced to a distributor problem the team lost a certain amount of time trying to remember the firing order for the new cap. By 20 hours they were back to eighth place. The engine was running ever weaker with failing fuel pressure and spluttering with burnt exhaust valves; but despite an agonising stop on the circuit when Ray Mallock had to regenerate fuel pressure, the car plodded on with all fingers crossed and finally took seventh place, the fourth group C car, behind five Porsches and a Ferrari 512BB. It was a great achievement which could only bode well for the following year.

Lack of finance was however beginning to tell and Pace were unable to keep supporting a complete race team. Both cars were out at Spa on a shoestring budget in September. The Downe car qualified thirteenth and 003 eighteenth. In the race 003 blew its engine at mid-distance but 004 once again kept going to finish eleventh, but seventh in Group C, enough to clinch third place overall in the Endurance Championship

Nimrod 004 on its way to seventh place at Le Mans 1982. Taxi sign was taller than that on 003 and the portholes became detached.

Nimrod 004 passing the Le Mans pits.

Celebrating their well-earned seventh at Le Mans, 004's crew acknowledge the applause – doors have been removed. Simon Phillips (left), Ray Mallock and Mike Salmon (right) are driven round by Richard Williams.

behind Porsche and Rondeau, but ahead of such established names as Lola, Ford and March.

The Downe Nimrod turned out once more in 1982 and that was the Brands Hatch 1000Km for the Drivers Championship; for this the International Construction company, Bovis, had decided to put a toe in the sponsorship water and were to be seen on the Nimrod for the first time. Mallock rewarded them by qualifying twelfth fastest on what was patently an unsuitable track for the heavy car. The race started in extremely wet conditions and had to be restarted following an accident between two Ford C-100s; Ray Mallock and Mike Salmon kept the Nimrod on the island and had run as high as sixth place before finally coming home ninth. It was a remarkable first season for Lord Downe's team with four starts, four finishes and a championship third; a tribute to Richard Williams' team.

Over the winter of 1982/3, the Nimrod financial situation worsened

For the final race of 1982, the Downe team negotiated some sponsorship from Bovis, the start of greater things to come. The front wing was tried to reduce understeer on the tight circuit.

with no sponsorship and Pace unable to help further; Robin Hamilton took over 100 per cent control and set off on his own to seek American sponsorship for the IMSA series. The first round was in Daytona for the 24-hour race where a single entry for 003 was suddenly increased by 002 rapidly flown from Fauld when Hamilton concluded a deal with organiser and the race sponsors, Pepsi, to have the car entered as the Pepsi Challenger, to be driven by none other than A. J. Foyt with Darrell Waltrip and Tiff Needell while Lynn St James, Drake Olson and John Graham drove 003. Minor troubles affected practice and they started twelfth and thirteenth on the grid. In the race Foyt had 002 as high as fifth, but after four hours a loose sump baffle plate caused internal injuries and the car was out; 003 had been pushed off in the early stages, but reached seventh before a baffle plate failure stopped that one too.

Hamilton went on to Miami where a rainstorm reduced the race to a mere 27 laps. Nimrod 002 ran quite well in the conditions but finished outside the top six.

At the Sebring 12-hour race Drake Olson and the team recorded its best ever result with a fine fifth place with Lynn St James and Reggie Smith. The other car went off the road early on. Road Atlanta saw Olson qualify seventh but a tyre deflation took them into the Armco and out of the race.

Subsequently chasis 002 was sold to Jack Miller and 003 was left in America, static for almost a year while Nimrod was sadly wound up; it had been an ambitious project to create a full-scale team but the lack of finance was against it. The great achievement was to leave behind the basis of Aston's return to motor racing, a story we hope is not yet finished.

Over the 1982/3 winter other work had seen Lord Downe's car receive new bodywork through the work of Ray Mallock, and Bovis was to become the major sponsor of that car; it was hoped to get 005 into the team as well but there wasn't enough money available to run two cars. Accordingly after much wind tunnel work on a ¼-scale model, Ray was convinced he had a shape that was more slippery and with greater downforce; early testing at Silverstone saw the car attain a more competitive 1 minute 21.9 seconds.

Meanwhile Steve O'Rourke, Pink Floyd's road manager and regular competitor in historic and Supersports races, had signed up Len Bailey to produce an Aston-powered successor to his Ford C-100, which was shortly to be axed by Ford. This was to be a much lighter car than the Nimrod and would use a stressed version of the Aston engine; accordingly Tickford redesigned the front end for direct chassis attachment and lightened the unit with aluminium liners with Nikasil coatings. The car was built by Michael Cane in Guildford; he had earlier had the task of maintaining O'Rourke's other racing machinery including a BMW M1 which had run in 1982 Endurance events.

The first 1983 race at Silverstone 1000Km saw Mallock/Salmon qualify in fifteenth place at 1 minute 22.7 seconds and O'Rourke's car with Jeff Allam and Tiff Needell co-driving clock 1 minute 24.45 seconds, a useful start for the EMKA, named after O'Rourke's record company.

The EMKA suffered an early set-back in the race pitting after the second lap with a misfire, losing five laps while a distributor cap was

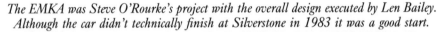

The EMKA was Steve O'Rourke's project with the overall design executed by Len Bailey. Although the car didn't technically finish at Silverstone in 1983 it was a good start.

*Now in full Bovis colours on its Mallock-revised bodywork, 004 Nimrod finished seventh –
its only result in an unlucky year.*

replaced, and a further five laps half an hour later to trace a still evident
misfire; but they sorted the car out and it ran regularly until the end,
gradually picking up places; it should have been awarded twelfth place
but a hub broke on its final lap and it never crossed the line. The
Downe car started at around tenth place moving up to seventh at mid-
distance which it held to the end despite losing some of its front
bodywork on an errant hare.

Le Mans was next on the agenda and Ray Mallock's winter work was
instantly justified after the practice sessions. In 1982 the fastest lap
recorded by a Rondeau in the race was 3 minutes 36 seconds; 1983
practice saw Mallock better that with 3 minutes 35.9 seconds and
qualify in sixteenth place, first of the non-turbos, and reach 213mph
down the Mulsanne straight. Mike Salmon was once again co-driver
but American Steve Earle replaced Simon Phillips. In the EMKA Tiff
Needell was twenty-sixth fastest with 3 minutes 42.23 seconds sharing
with O'Rourke and Nick Faure. Both cars carried evidence of Pace
sponsorship but in comparison with the previous year it was really only a
token effort.

In the race all did not go well for the Nimrod. Although the team was up to twelfth place after the first hour, the battery was getting overcharged; with battery and alternator changes they kept going, but then had to strip a gearbox to replace a selector fork. Then just after mid-night the electrical problems caused a wiring fire under the facia which burnt through petrol and oil gauge lines; by the time Salmon had limped the car back to the pits a lot of oil had been lost. This was repaired and at 1.30 am they were in thirty-first place, climbing gradually up to thirteenth by 9 am, but then the engine cried enough, having run without oil some hours previously, and that was that.

The EMKA fared a little better. A holed radiator, a broken rear wishbone, replacing hub bearings, all cost them a lot of time in the pits, but they kept going to the end to finish seventeenth. Obviously the EMKA had some potential; it was down to 900Kg in Le Mans trim (against the Nimrod's 987Kg) but it needed further development. Sadly O'Rourke too had been unable to find a major sponsor and the car was not raced in 1984 despite Cane's efforts over the following winter.

At Le Mans 1983 the EMKA driven by O'Rourke, Needell and Nick Faure did very well to finish seventeenth after many stops.

The Downe team decided to return to Spa again but the original faithful 1982 engine was all they had left and that dropped a con-rod with just an hour to run when the team were running in seventh position. At the final event for the Bovis-Downe team, the Brands Hatch 1000Km started in torrential rain; by the time the weather had cleared the car was running in ninth place. Drying conditions saw others pass and they were down to twelfth when the crown wheel and pinion failed. It was the end of an unlucky season which saw the car looking much more competitive, but fate, which had been so kind in 1982, had swung the other way.

The winter of 1983/4 saw little development due to lack of substantial funds, although Bovis would continue to cover the running of the Downe team. In December privateer John Cooper bought car 005 to campaign in IMSA and group C racing. With a little help from AMLNA the Downe team decided to join John Cooper's entry at Daytona; Ray Mallock was to be partnered by Drake Olson and British privateer John Sheldon joined the team. John Cooper's car, in British

Le Mans 1983 wasn't kind to the Bovis/Downe team; electrical problems caused a loss of oil and the engine expired.

Racing Green, was driven by Bob Evans and Paul Smith. Neither car had an uneventful run, but both reached the end of the 24-hour race, 005 in seventh place after a slow and cautious run and 004 in sixteenth after overheating during many laps running under the pace car system; first wheel bearings suffered and then head gaskets. Despite his Daytona success John Cooper then opted out of running the Nimrod in further American events, and sold 005 to AMLNA who immediately added it to the Downe team as a second car in the Bovis colours. Moreover this was to be turbocharged as fast as possible and all its bodywork was to be in Kevlar before the first outing at Silverstone.

While the Aston Martin Tickford team had their turbo experience with the Lagonda, Bulldog and the Tickford Capri to draw upon, there just wasn't the development time to get the installation right. While it was a superb sight to see the two cars at Silverstone, the team was in poor spirits after continued turbo gasket troubles, and engine changes. Sadly 005 was soon in trouble during the race and retired after a little more than an hour; 004 with Mike Salmon and John Sheldon and

For 1984 Nimrod 005 joined the team and ran with turbochargers at Silverstone where neither that car nor old faithful 004 finished.

Exciting line-up at Le Mans with the two Bovis sponsored quasi-works entries. It was a cruel stroke of fate that took both cars out at the same moment with such tragic results.

Richard Attwood were running strongly at a predetermined 1 minute 27 seconds when a dropped valve intervened.

The decision had to be taken to abandon turbocharging for Le Mans, only four weeks away, and the team concentrated on getting two normally aspirated cars in top trim. They were determined to do well in the 25th anniversary year of the 1959 victory. The lightweight car (comparatively speaking) was straight away very impressive in practice, recording 3 minutes 33.14 seconds; this was Jaguar's first year back at Le Mans and the Aston team was out to beat them, even to the extent of using qualifying tyres and an 'expendable' engine, allowed to be run to 7200rpm. The ploy worked and 005 qualified tenth fastest, some three seconds ahead of the first Jaguar and fastest of the non-turbo cars.

The race itself was to prove a disaster. Both cars were running well with 005 splitting the Jaguars around eighth place after three hours, and 004 around twelfth. Then as dusk was gathering John Sheldon, driving 004, had a left rear tyre deflate at the Mulsanne Kink; it was probable

221

that this had happened earlier on the straight and centrifugal force had supported the car until the moment came to turn into the flat-out kink. At over 200mph the tail snapped round, the car charged the barrier on the inside and started to break up; the centre section cartwheeled down the top of the Armco and a piece of the front suspension killed a marshal.

The car finally came to rest having caught fire in the process and Sheldon had to be dragged clear. While this had been going on, Palmer's Porsche 956 had been closing on the Nimrod; he hadn't seen the start of the incident taking place beyond the kink but he had seen enough dust in the air to make him brake heavily. Drake Olson, in the Nimrod 005 just behind Palmer, had to decide either to ram the Porsche or try and get round; he chose the latter course but got onto the stony edge of the track and spun down the straight, hitting the barrier, to stop not far beyond the blazing remains of the other team car. Olson was only shaken but Sheldon was badly burned; thanks to swift action he was taken quickly to Tours hospital and a week later was back at the East Grinstead Burns Hospital, thankfully on the way to recovery.

It was a cruel piece of coincidence that both the cars should be on the same bit of track at the same time. That was inevitably the end of the team's 1984 season; 004 was written off, but 005 was put back together in race trim for an uncertain future.

It is to be hoped that the Downe team will be out on the tracks again in 1985 with a new car, along with the Aston-powered carbon fibre Cheetah built for Swiss exponent Chuck Gremiger. But, meanwhile, the last three years of Aston Martin in modern racing have been a very effective promotion, particularly in France, and lessons are still being learnt that could benefit the production cars.

Chapter Thirteen

Once more into the breach

Not only was America the most prolific market, it was also the most profitable, thanks to the otherwise lamented steady down-turn of the pound. This not only enabled AII to back the instrumentation project, but also to help the 1984 Nimrod-Aston team; and there was also a steady flow of other interesting machinery passing through the dealership side of Greenwich. Everything in the garden should have been rosy; AML should have been earning a steady income from US exports, AMLNA was earning enough for AII to fund the more expensive development projects and AII would still have some left over to repay their investment reasonably quickly.

At this moment the depressed state of the tanker market was to intervene. While the Livanos interests are solidly based on the ownership of the majority of their large and successful fleet which operates in divers business areas, Titan was a young, highly geared shipping and broking company dependant to a considerable extent on the movement of bulk cargoes in rented tankers; it only needs a few hiccoughs of oil dropping in price on the high seas, or a tanker being unable to dock during someone else's war, to consume the small percentage margins.

As Pace had found before in a comparable high turnover small margin business, Titan too found the money going out faster than it came in, but for too long a period to withstand; while Pace had found the bottom of the trough and could see the way ahead to trade gradually out of the situation, Titan was literally in deeper waters. Astonishingly, given the company's past history, AML was actually funding its parents' problems. The lack of cash travelling from West to East was nearly too much for the Newport Pagnell finances to bear and trading was very tight during the summer of 1984 with cars for America unable to be shipped.

In response to pressure from AML and its AII partners, the Papanicolaous' shares were recovered to give control to the Livanos company; 75 per cent was thus owned by the Livanos family interests and the balance by Victor Gauntlett. AII ceased to be a factor in Aston's life and a new company was formed, Aston Martin Lagonda Group Ltd, owners of both American and British interests.

What had looked a bleak prospect for a short time for the customarily resilient company had turned out remarkably well. With Victor Gauntlett remaining at the helm again with a vested interest, and with solid backing, the future looks brighter. But the days had long gone when Aston Martin could be allowed to be a drain on anyone's resources and it became necessary to reduce the output from five to four cars a week to reduce the capital tied up on the Newport Pagnell site, both in cars being built and the stock required; sadly this meant some redundancies and 60 of the firm's, then 390, employees had to move on to leave behind a leaner, tighter and more efficient ship, able to build on firmer footings.

While this book has been essentially concerned with the V-8 Aston Martin, no development story can be complete without reference to the company's general situation, as it has so often affected the rate of progress. Work will continue on improving the general level of comfort and mechanical refinement and the market has shown that there is still plenty of interest in that bespoke exclusivity that only Newport Pagnell offers to the world's discerning owners of fine cars. While the recent succession of owners has each reckoned to displace the V-8 within two or three years of their takeovers, there is still plenty of life left in it yet, and the Lagonda will probably outlast it. It is the recent upturn in V-8 demand that has allowed the company to defer the introduction of a new car once more; the 1986 date announced in summer 1983 is likely to move on to at least 1988. I hope I can look forward to taking part in sustaining the V-8 until then and that there will be every reason to update this book.